One Man's Walk with God
Preparing for Trials and Fears

Jeremy B. Strang

One Man's Walk with God
Preparing for Trials and Fears

Contents

Thank you to my mighty God for saving my soul and revealing Himself to me. Oh, that I might always look to Him to be my most precious and greatest need of my life. Thank you to my dear wife and children who show me patience, grace and mercy, although I know I do not deserve it.

I also thank all my brothers and sisters in Christ who have read this book and given me your feedback. Special thanks to Jeff Bys for writing the foreword and to Charaki Yeomans for your editorial comments and recommendations.

"For now we see in a mirror dimly, but then face to face. Now I know in part; then I shall know fully, even as I have been fully known."

1 Corinthians 13:12

Recommendations

"*Grape juice, apple juice, orange juice or another type of juice, are all the result of pressure being applied to the outside until what is inside flows out. Strangely enough, you can't obtain olive oil from apples or apple juice from grapes. Each of these when under pressure reveal exactly what they 'are' inside. When God transforms a life by His grace, the person's very nature is changed by the indwelling nature of Almighty God. Jeremy Strang has undergone that spiritual metamorphous. How do I know? Because of what flows out of him. Out of the abundance of the heart the mouth speaks, or in this case he writes. He writes about a love affair with his God and Savior. I pray as you read that you too will fall in love with the one who is 'The Desire of All Nations, The King of kings, The Lord of lords, The Maker of Heaven and Earth, the altogether Lovely One, and our glorious Redeemer'. Eternity will not be sufficient to grasp the magnitude and greatness of our God.*"

– David Ravenhill, Preacher, Teacher and Writer

"*Written with a heart to edify believers, this book will encourage you to communion more with God and thirst and hunger after Him. I recommend it. For those who spend time with God truly will become more like Him.*"

– Greg Gordon, Founder of Sermon Index

"I see such passion, such as one whom has been touched by the Lord Himself, going strongly yet humbly, before our God, sometimes tearfully before Him. With such passion in his heart, thus for a steadfast and unshakable relationship, and bearing the very heart and thoughts wide open before God. How pleasing this is to our Lord and the very thing our Father desires, communication with the deep thoughts and praises of his child. I see the very representation of the heart of David here. I believe this book is the working of the Holy Spirit to draw us closer to our Lord and to pursue Him with our whole heart. For it is there we shall find him."

– Lynn Clark, Christian

"What an encouragement to listen in as Jeremy Strang speaks to the One his soul loves. As I hung on each word, I got the real sense that Jeremy communicates out of the overflow of his heart. As we serve God in dark places throughout a world that is not our home, it is a blessing of God to be encouraged by such men. My prayer is that God might deepen your sense of awe in Him, your love for Him, and your service to Him as you read this beautiful work."

– Jeff Bys, Missionary in Kenya

To any true seeker, believer, and follower of Jesus Christ, Jeremy Strang's words encapsulate the heart felt yearning, constant search, inner struggles, and rich spiritual blessings that accompany the ever-deepening relationship Christ wants with each of us. As a fellow believer my faith is enriched, and so will yours be. Read on and be blessed!"

– Steve Shullanberger, Pastor and Preacher

"In the spirit of the Psalmists in the Scriptures and the Puritans in The Valley of Vision, Jeremy Strang writes as a man who has been gripped by the grace of God. Each chapter is filled with prayers that reckon with the sinfulness that yet remains in the hearts of even the redeemed as their hearts are laid bare and are confronted with the pure, unapproachable holiness of God in His Word. Yet, while bringing such grievous realities to light before God, Jeremy Strang quickly looks to Christ, the One who stands before God with our names written on His hands and ever lives to intercede for us. In short, my brother teaches us again in this book, when our devotional lives feel dried up and our fruits are few, that our gaze must ever be on Christ all our days. Only in Him will we once again see the truth of that beloved hymn, "Our sins, they are many. His mercy is more." I heartily recommend this book."

– Ryan Rutan, Christian and Moody Bible Student

"If your desire is for a closer walk with the Lord, this book is a must read. The love this author shows for Jesus flows off the pages in a beautiful form of poetry and prayers to the Lord. I too not only hung on each word but wept as I understood the

love Jeremy has for Jesus. The honesty, humility and passion written on these pages is an encouragement to give up all for our precious and most worthy Savior. "

– Linda Mann, Christian

"I've known Jeremy Strang for quite some time and read his books, read his blogs and speak with Him regularly; he is my friend and brother in Christ. So to some extent, I've seen his passion for God and understand when he writes a book such as this. If I could focus on one single goal of Jeremy through his writings, it is that you would seek the Lord and know Him more and more. At the end of our time when it is all said and done, we all must have Christ. This is where our lives begin and this is where it ends, in Christ. So seek the Lord today that you may know and be found in Him as Paul describes in Philippians 3:7-11." Christ blessings,

– Warren Judge, Christian and Layman Preacher

"One Man's Walk with God reads like a conversation between the author and his Heavenly Father. From a humble and sincere heart, Jeremy writes out of a desire to draw himself and others closer to our Lord and Savior."

– Charaki Yeomans, Christian

Purpose and design of this book

In this day of technology, political narratives, self-absorption and narcissistic impulses, it seems that the world all-around is imploding. People are growing exceedingly anxious and fearful, and experiencing trials in increasing measure. As darkness seems to be manifesting all over the planet and in every area known to man, so many are feeling completely hopeless. However, for the true Christian, these things should come as no surprise; sadly though, many believers seem to be struggling with how to relieve their fears and continue forward, navigating the dangerous waters of the daily unknown.

In this book, *One Man's Walk with God*, author Jeremy B. Strang brings to the pages a personal approach regarding our need to authentically walk with God, especially as it pertains to preparing for the many trials and uncertain fears. Whether you are in the throes of personal darkness and various types of difficulties, or you are seemingly on the mountain top of life, you will want to read this intimate account. Each chapter is presented in the form of a letter and close conversation with God, and applicable for the reader desiring to grow in the faith.

It is Jeremy's hope and prayer that you will be edified and challenged, given peace and freedom, and most importantly, encouraged to walk closely with the Creator. Proceeds from the purchase of this book benefits Jeff and Stephanie Bys, AFM missionaries in Kenya. Learn more: AFM.ngo

"The world is not spinning out of control; in fact, not one atom or despot or demon acts in any respect to hinder the fulfillment of what God has eternally ordained. To know this God, and better to be known by him (Gal. 4:9a), is to enter into the security and confidence of a lifetime of trust in his never-failing arms."[1]

---

[1] Bruce A. Ware, *God's Greater Glory: The Exalted God of Scripture and the Christian Faith*, p. 15

Foreword

I first heard the name Jeremy Strang shortly after arriving in Kenya. It was December of 2016, and after years of having an unquenchable desire to leave the U.S. for Africa, and through much answered prayer, God had now seen fit to bring me to the unknown in Kenya along with my wife and our seven youngest children. By God's providence, we settled in the small village of Kaya and out of our God-given passion to care for orphans and needy children, our family-built Mercy Home. Now approaching four years since our arrival, I can only say with even greater surety than before, that God is good. Through every trial, including being attacked by an angry mob led by prosperity gospel *"pastors"* intending to chase us out of Kenya and take over our project, and even being jailed, God has been so good and gracious to us. He has provided for our every need and we would not want to change a thing. He has drawn near to us as we have drawn near to Him (James 4:8).

Through everything, God has continued to provide for the needs of our growing family of over 100 children. God has provided for us to establish a primary school to be a blessing to our community, including providing for the church we have planted in our village. God has provided through Gospel preaching, souls who are being saved. God also provided a great friend, brother, and encourager through Jeremy. Having heard about us while we were in the air on the way to Africa, Jeremy soon contacted me *out of the blue* (from my perspective); but what a blessing God has given us in Jeremy.

Even before I finally got the chance to meet him face to face in 2019, I had already felt a closeness to him that can only be explained as of the Lord. I thank God for all of His loving provision to us, His children. But no matter where we are, or what we do, I can say that most importantly, God has provided a Lamb (John 1:29).

It is this Lamb, this mediator, this Savior Jesus Christ that we can, and must, place our entire dependence upon His merits, not having any of our own. And God is faithful to keep His promise to save sinners, among whom I consider myself to be the greatest. We can do nothing but be in awe of our God who seeks us when we do not seek Him (Romans 3:11), who became sin for us so that we may become His righteousness (2 Corinthians 5:21) and who died for us while we were still sinners (Romans 5:8). It is this King of kings and Lord of lords that we owe everything, even our lives. To serve Jesus is no sacrifice, it is the only sensible thing to do; it is the greatest privilege. We can say with Paul that *"to live is Christ, and to die is gain."* We have absolutely nothing to lose. In Christ, we gain everything. A life lived for ourselves is a life wasted. It is only a life spent walking with God, in Christ, that has any value.

For you have delivered my soul from death, yes, my feet from falling, that I may walk before God in the light of life.
Psalm 56:13

I believe what Jeremy has beautifully captured in the pages of this book is a personal approach to live life authentically *"before God."* *Coram Deo* is the Latin phrase in the Vulgate in this Psalm meaning *"before the face of God"* or *"in the presence of God*". It is as R.C. Sproul put it, *"to live one's entire life in the presence of God, under the authority of God, to the glory of God."* I trust you will find in these pages what I have found from my dear brother Jeremy; an encouragement, a motivation, and a call to live life *coram Deo.*

Jeff R. Bys, Missionary in Kenya and Pastor of Mercy Baptist Church, Kenya

Section One

He Satisfies

"For He satisfies the longing soul, and the hungry soul He fills with good things."

Psalm 107:9

Chapter One

How shall I come to You?

"Guard your steps when you go to the house of God. To draw near to listen is better…"

Ecclesiastes 5:1

Oh Lord my God, for how shall I come to You? You are holy, righteous, just and good; apart from You I am not. And yet for your namesake, the love of the world,[1] and for my life and eternal spirit, You have reckoned and accounted to me through Christ alone, His righteousness – giving unto me new life and joy unspeakable. Oh what deep and eternal peace I have been granted by the powerfully true work of Your grace.[2] Oh that freeing grace of Your dear Son's propitiation[3] in justifying me, and suffering the wrath that was due to me[4] – only by my precious Lord and Savior Jesus Christ. Oh what light You have caused to shine upon my darkened soul. Praise be to you Lord God that while I was yet

---

[1] John 3:16
[2] Ephesians 2:8, 9
[3] Romans 3:25
[4] John 3:36; Romans 3:9-18, 3:23, 6:23

destitute and a sinner through and through, a man of ill repute, vile and uncaring, a man of shame and evil, You first loved me.[1] Oh what amazing and unfathomable grace You have powerfully worked and effectually given me. This new heart is feeling and pliable, regenerated and justified, nothing short of miraculous, and this without any works of my own. Oh Your grace! How great is Your love that I *should be called*[2] Your child?

Oh Lord my God, for how shall I come and speak to You? In the one respect I cannot but approach You in any other way than with deep and profound reverence, just as *"the Preacher"* has said, *"Guard your steps when you go to the house of God. To draw near to listen is better than to offer the Sacrifice of fools, for they do not know that they are doing evil."*[3] And yet this would not be reverent enough…

However, in another respect, I feel like the little child calling for his Abba Father, like the naïve and innocent, like the weak and inept, like the child needing to be picked up and embraced by You, the Almighty and omnipotent God. And yet this too does not explain it all…

And yet further still, I feel like the violently desperate, the passionate and yet weak, the relentless and yet wholly dependent, like one who seeks to lay hold of Your promises[4] – like one who was formerly lame and now running, like the one formerly deaf and now joyously hearing, like the

---

[1] 1 John 4:19
[2] 1 John 3:1
[3] Ecclesiastes 5:1-3
[4] Matthew 11:12; Luke 16:16

formerly blind and now lit up by new vision, like Lazarus who came out of the grave[1] and like David who danced before You.[2] Oh, to shout it from the mountaintops and spend all of my days at Your foot, looking to that empty cross, that place by which You ransomed and redeemed my starving soul; oh, to dwell with You forever!

> *"As a deer pants for flowing streams so pants my soul for You, O God. My soul thirsts for God, for the living God, when shall I come and appear before God? My tears have been my food day and night, while they say to me all the day long, 'Where is your God?' These things I remember, as I remember, as I pour out my soul; how I would go with the throng and lead them in procession to the house of God with glad shouts and songs of praise, a multitude keeping festival."[3]*

And though these two decades have passed by so quickly, I feel as if I could talk to You like the babe who has recently learned to talk and please his parents – so much to say, so much amazement, and yet so very much in need of listening and learning.

Oh Lord my God, you know that quite possibly the greatest area still lacking self-control is in the words of my mouth. For I find it simple to be controlled when I take time to think, to write, and to do so when no one is around is easy; however, it is often more difficult to be aware amid spontaneous and busy times, when the mind is on other things, words come spewing

---

[1] John 11:43

[2] 2 Samuel 6:14

[3] Psalm 42:1-4

forth from the '*old man*' – and this in the front of dearly loved ones. Oh how my lips need yet more discipline. As Your Spirit has reminded me, it is not the tongue alone, but the very heart[1] – that old nature – that is in need of being put to death.[2] If You will judge every idle word that I have spoken, how then shall I come before You? You know how there are times when I speak forth evil against my fellow man,[3] and how there are times I bless your holy name and this with the very same mouth.[4] Oh Lord, how much I am in need like Your prophet Isaiah: "*Woe is me! For I am lost; for I am a man of unclean lips, and I dwell in the midst of a people of unclean lips...*" Lord, may I see You the same – "*...for my eyes have seen the King, the LORD of hosts!*"[5] Lord, touch these lips of mine, for if not, how shall I come and speak with you? May I never forget, and may I grow more deeply in the reality that You are my greatest of needs. For in you alone is all the power, wisdom and truth alone.

Oh Lord my God, how shall I come and approach You? – Lord, You alone know me. You know me better than I know myself, and yet, with all my weakness, failures, sins and enmity past, You show me mercy each and every day.[6] And if it should be that You tarry, and should You sustain me another two decades, I hope and pray that these things will

---

1 Matthew 15:18; Luke 6:45
2 Romans 8:13
3 Titus 3:2
4 James 3:9 (3:1-12)
5 Isaiah 6:5-7
6 Lamentations 3:22, 23

continue to grow and mature; that they will be fanned into a bright burning flame.

Lord, I hope and pray that these letters would be pleasing in Your sight and make Your glory known among those who may read this in the future. May You be glorified; please Lord, sanctify me unto becoming more and more like Your dear Son, my Lord and Savior. Only You know, oh Lord, if these things, these thoughts, these mere words, have taken root within me; please Lord God, if in these things I am false, then make them come alive unto me and grow them forevermore.

Lord, apprehend my affections and mold me into a vessel of honor suitable for Your glory, Your worship and Your honor.

Amen.

"The first and chief need of our Christian life is, Fellowship with God."[1]

---

[1] Andrew Murray, *The Deeper Christian Life and Other Writings*, p. 3

Chapter Two

My greatest need

"And the Word became flesh and dwelt among us, and we have seen His glory, glory as of the only Son from the Father, full of grace and truth."

John 1:14

Oh mighty Lord, I praise You that the *morning star*,[1] He who existed from the beginning,[2] has risen in and upon my heart. Oh the *unsearchable riches of Christ*,[3] the depths, beauties, richness of worth, oh so far beyond my comprehension is the infinite value of Your Son; and yet you have made Yourself to be known to me, although I was completely blind to see and dumb to understand, You have made my vision clear and my mind sharp to understand; that You are my greatest of needs. For in your grace, mercy and

---

[1] 2 Peter 1:19
[2] John 1:1
[3] Job 28:13

great love, You have taught me to trust You and recognize my eternal condition without You.

Prior to having You as my treasured joy and everlasting prince of peace, I was ignorant and dead, grasping firm the lies of Satan and steeped in my own narcissistic and deceptive heart.[1] I believed, as all fallen men are born to think, that my nature was not that bad and that in some way, in some strength, or by some religious duties, I could be found favorable to attain some form of grand abyss when I die – what damnable foolishness was this prison of thought.

However, now having been granted new life, and the binding darkness of melancholy having melted away, after these beginning years of being sanctified and tried over and over, and after being taught Your Scriptures by the conviction and training of Your Holy Spirit, I see the utter folly of such thinking. However, I have not forgotten, nor do I ever want to forget, the reason such godless thinking exists. Lord, let me not forget and wander from You, or care not for my fellow man, or think I am more special than I am – may it never be.

Lord, I remember that this was not all revealed to me in the blink of an eye. I praise You mighty God for Your longsuffering and patient training of my mind to understand greater and greater realties of Your nature, character and eternal will for me, both for the present and for eternity future. Oh, to see, to taste and experience, the riches of Christ and to never forget Him as my greatest of needs. I can only imagine that if the thief on the cross had been left alive and brought

---

[1] Jeremiah 17:9

down after recognizing Jesus, and if he were to have taught on the workings of grace, would they not have been limited? Yet because he was limited in knowledge, does this diminish his testimony or his salvation? Lord, not one bit would he have been lost or denied! For him to have had the understandings and workings of Your perfect balance, Your grace, Your calling to repentance, Your propitiation, justification and imputation, would it not have taken him years of study, reading and training – in both righteousness and sanctification? Surely, oh Lord, You know!

Lord, I pray that I will never forget how You have powerfully redeemed my soul and have patiently worked in me these last years. Oh that I would show patience towards those who have yet to experience and understand such freeing grace and freedom found in absolutely knowing that salvation is a work completely of You. Hallelujah, for You have shown me the foothills of such wonderful glory – oh, for what could I ever bring to You as a gift that you would exchange in pardon for my depraved nature, or what can I add to the *unsearchable riches* of Christ? Absolutely, ten thousand times over, nothing!

Lord, I also ask of You, never let me become lax or lazy, or sleepy and dull regarding the faith You have given me. I ask and pray that You would continue to grant me a growing desire to both walk with You, knowing You[1] in greater measure, and to be laboring to do Your good works that You have prepared for me to do; and not this alone, but to strive to

---

[1] Jeremiah 9:23-25

work out my salvation with fear and trembling,[1] making my *calling sure,*[2] and to *plow up my fallow ground.*[3] Oh Lord, give me such balance so that I am not found tipping the scales – on the one hand full of zeal without knowledge whereby I am boasting in my works, nor let me be found the other side neither, full of knowledge and rote words with no conviction, loveless and without joy, nor failing to do the works of righteousness, true religion and obedience. Lord, may it never be. Let me never treat You by mere thought and mental ascent, but grow me ever more that I might be diligent, resolved and joyous to carry out Your will – produce the fruits of Your Spirit, to love, seek to be holy and help to fulfill the great commission. What joy indeed!

Over these last years since Your merciful hand rescued my very life, I still find I must ask myself, and often others that I meet, these questions: *Do I in truth, deep down and honest, even have a desire to really know and follow You? Or am I fooling myself being taken up with rote language and happy in mere discussion about You? Have I fallen into meaningless actions of the flesh alone, such as being morally-good and making attendance at some building once per week, whereby I am satisfying some curiosities and religious carnality rather than truly desiring You? Am I really desirous to walk with You? Or do the cares of this world and its system guide my paths? Furthermore, do I even care, or dare, to ask such questions?* For more than I would like, or would like to admit, I find myself in the routines and toils of the day, dull, dry and

---

[1] Philippians 2:12
[2] 2 Peter 1:10
[3] Jeremiah 4:3; Hosea 10:12

doing the very things I wish I would not, for the good I wish to do, I do not do.[1]

Lord, I find that too often, like one who should be past the milk, I must yet again come to the awareness of the truth of my inner heart and come to the truth of these questions. If I cannot here admit my state, I find that everything else in due time falls. For if I am not building upon The Foundational Cornerstone, the collapse into sin is inevitable. And although Your grace abounds, should I let sin continue to sink me, should I continue in life turning a blind eye with no resolve, lacking the daily desire to grow in You? – NO, never! Let me not take my sin lightly, nor be found using grace as an excuse for my personal disobedience, nor let me be found wondering and aimless in spirit, but oh Lord show me to continue building, with great desire and resolve, upon Christ Jesus.

Having said this, I then find I have only three choices in my response to the questions above: First, I can forget these altogether, however for the Christian this is not at all wise. Second, I can admit I am not really desiring to know You. Or third, I can admit I do indeed desire to know You and am dry and in need. If my response is like the second, and much like the first, I am greatly in need of being awakened to the truth in hearing clearly my condition and in understanding the consequences should I answer unwise. For I can respond here in either choosing to turn away from You (never let it be), or I can turn to You and ask You for such desire, a desire with which to begin, a desire to know You. As with the third response, it is the same, to again seek You and Your wisdom

---

[1] Romans 7:15

in asking You for an ever-increasing desire to walk intimately with You. Lord, You know my thoughts and my true answers.

Oh Lord, that you would work in me to will and to work for your good pleasure,[1] that I might continue to walk near You, with my sights set and mind resolved that You indeed are my greatest of needs – and this not in mere words or thoughts, but in truth and reality, both in the temporal and the eternal life to come. Why would carnal men not get angry at the sound of Your Son's name? Why would they not curse by His name? They make for themselves great enmity against You as they walk in their pride and ignorance, denying and cursing You, their Creator, the one true God. The course of fallen men grievously opposes You, I having been just as bad as the very worst kind, have also taken pleasure in the flesh, denying Your truths, denying Your very Son – may I never be found in such a drastic state again! Oh praise Your holy name, for although I was but lost, now I am found![2] For just as the Apostle Paul has said, *"The saying is trustworthy and deserving of full acceptance, that Christ Jesus came into the world to save sinners, of whom I am the foremost."*[3]

For You have *"bestowed on Him the name that is above every name, so that at the name of Jesus every knee should bow, in heaven and on earth and under the earth, and every tongue confess that Jesus Christ is Lord, to"* Your glory.[4] For by You, Jesus is the Cornerstone *"and there is salvation in no one else,*

---

[1] Philippians 2:13
[2] Luke 15:32
[3] 1 Timothy 1:15
[4] Philippians 2:9-11

for there is no other name under heaven given men by which we must be saved."[1] For even in men's rebellion, denial and perverse usage of Your great name they give testimony to Your reality, truth and sovereign rule even though they remain blind, dead, unrepentant and under Your wrath.[2] Awake them, oh Lord, just as You have me, awake them to the truths of Christ and His pardoning propitiation and sacrificial agape.

And as for the one, Lord, faking true faith, awake this one as well, for the sake of Your dear Son, for Jesus Himself is never enough to those who profess and are yet ignorant of regeneration. But as for me, knowing You and Jesus Christ whom You have sent, is indeed eternal life.[3] Lord help me to continue to advance, walking the narrow and joy-filled path, that I may never boast in myself, my work, my status, my situation in life, but that my boast would be in knowing You[4] and that I may rejoice that my name is written in heaven.[5] God, Your *"kingdom does not consist in words but in power."*[6] As You know Lord, I was *"dwelling in darkness"* and I have *"seen a great light."*[7]

---

[1] Acts 4:11-2

[2] John 3:36

[3] John 17:3

[4] Jeremiah 9:23-25

[5] Luke 10:20

[6] 1 Corinthians 4:20

[7] Matthew 4:16

Oh Lord my God, You are light[1] and You promise that whoever follows Your Son does not walk in darkness.[2] You have granted to me *"all things that pertains to life and godliness,"*[3] so teach me how to use and to walk in that which you have given me. Grow me Lord in true lasting personal piety, that I would treasure You and Your perfectly balanced scales, Your working and Your character. Amen.

---

[1] 1 John 1:5
[2] John 8:12
[3] 2 Peter 1:3

"The constant contemplation of the glory of Christ will give rest, satisfaction, and complacency to the souls of them who are exercised in that respect. Our minds are apt to be filled with a multitude of perplexed thoughts; fears, cares, dangers, distresses, passions and lusts, do make various impressions on the minds of men, filling them with disorder, darkness and confusion. But where the soul is fixed in its thoughts and contemplations on the glorious object, it will be brought into and kept in a holy, serene, spiritual frame. For, 'to be spiritually-minded is life and peace.' And this it does by taking off our hearts from all undue regard to all things below, in comparison of the great worth, beauty, and glory of what we are conversant with (see Phil. 3:7-11). A defect in this makes many of us strangers to a heavenly life, and to live beneath the spiritual refreshments and satisfactions that the gospel tenders to us."

"But it is from our own sloth and darkness that we do not enjoy more visits of this grace, and that the dawnings of glory do not more shine on our souls."[1]

---

[1] John Owen, *The Glory of Christ: His Office and Grace*, p. 48, 49

Chapter Three

Growing in the beauty of Your word

"Your word is a lamp to my feet and a light to my path."

Psalms 119:105

This morning, Father, my soul feels so carried, so lifted up, so highly exalted and close to You; so joyous that I cannot apply words to explain my greatly happy heart. Oh praises upon praises be unto You my God for ever and ever. Oh how sweet is Your word is to me;[1] I feel so lifted in Your love, joy and new mercies today, for it would be far better to continue this writing again later – for to worship You, in fellowship, *spirit and truth*,[2] to literally walk with You being shut up to You is by far the most excellent place I desire. Like the Apostle Paul said, *"…to depart and be with Christ, for that is far better."*[3] – what an amazing truth! You have given me such joy this day, I find it best here to step

---

[1] Psalms 119:103
[2] John 4:23-4
[3] Philippians 1:23

away from this and dwell intimately with You. May this take deeper root in me. Amen.

> *"He knew that the ultimate rest, blessedness, and satisfaction of the soul, is not in seeing the works of God, but the glory of God Himself."*[1]

Lord, it has been a few days since last picking up my pencil and coming to you in this fashion. I am again reminded through Your word that You are good regardless of my feelings and emotional tides. You tell me to draw near to You and You will draw near to me[2] – oh such a sweet promise should I comply. Oh Lord that I would only trust You and grow in Your word, that I would simply obey and leave the results in Your sovereign hands. For to the degree You make Yourself known to me, although obedience on my part to seek You, is as You know to be fitting for me during the season and day of my life.

I am further reminded that there is no sinless perfection with me, there is no one that I am the superior, thereby so very much am I needful of You and Your precious life giving word. Your word is a *"lamp"* and *"light"* unto me and the way in which I walk, needful in all my ways. Your word, Lord God, is not only "breathed out" by You, but it is sufficient for every aspect of my life; and because You are the inspiration of the Scriptures,[3] I also know that it is infallible, thereby giving me even more the reason to trust every iota. And although I may at times be feeling the painful toils resulting

---

[1] John Owen, *The Glory of Christ: His Office and Grace*, p. 58
[2] James 4:8
[3] 2 Timothy 3:16-17

from my fallen nature,[1] and may be temporary in my blinded unbelief in some aspect or another regarding Your promises and goodness, I know because of who You are and Your word, You will work in me that which is eternally best for me, according to Your great love and word. I am reminded that if it were not for Your grace and the propitiation of my dear Lord and Savior Christ Jesus, that amazing sacrificial love and imputation, I would yet be in a growing heap of sin so insurmountable that I would forever be undone because of my atrocities and enmity against You; and yet, even though I have been made new and given a new heart with new motives and desires, and shown such unconceivable love, I find myself still too often wrestling with fears and doubts; and if this were not enough, depression and anxiety desires to sink its arrows deep within, all while unbelief longs to persuade my heart away from Christ – *"Oh wretched man I am! Who will deliver me from this body of death?"* Thanks be to You through Your dear Son my Lord![2]

Praises be to You Lord God, maker of heaven and earth, that You have given me Your word – for Your word is a *lamp* unto me! And yet, regarding Your word, is this not the very place I too often forget? Although I know Your word is indeed the best for me, is this not where unbelief lays its attack and whispers in my ears that it is not for me? But, oh Lord, how can I not trust You, for You indeed not only have the words of eternal life,[3] but You are eternal life.[4] Thereby I ask You

---

[1] Genesis 3:17-19

[2] Romans 7:24, 25

[3] John 6:68

[4] John 17:3; 1 John 2:25

yet again, and ten thousand times over, help my unbelief[1] and continue to grow me in the beauty of Your word. Give me ears to hear, wisdom to understand, and a humble heart willingly obedient to apply the words that I may grow in patience, love and mercy. Lord, may Your strong arm be shown as You teach, reprove, correct and train me up in Your ways and will. May You increase my reverence of You and increase a measure of desire and love for Your word; grow an obedient resolve in me that I might be diligent to read, study, ponder, pray through and meditate upon Your word. Your word is vastly wonderful, and I can yet not even grasp the foothills of such realities.

As the fear of You is only the beginning of knowledge and wisdom,[2] may I also increase my awareness of a right and *strong confidence* in You. May I never forget the *fountain of life*,[3] which is Your promise for those who fear You. May Your word be forever branded and brought to my mind when trials and fears come to hunt me down. In light of Your inspired, sufficient and infallible word, help me to deeply understand and see with eternal eyes and to heed – "*Look carefully, then how you walk… making the best use of the time, because the days are evil.*"[4] How many are the distractions of this fallen world and my old-natured mind? – You know oh Lord.

---

[1] Mark 9:23-25

[2] Proverbs 1:7

[3] Proverbs 14:26, 27

[4] Ephesians 5:16, 16

If this were not enough for me to consider, then You remind me to ask, is not Jesus the word made flesh?[1] Is He not the fulfillment of the Law and Prophets?[2] So why Lord do I continue to be tempted with other desires? Is it not because of my lawless flesh, the *old-man* within still longing for carnality[3] and seeking to escape the *double-edged sword*[4] of Your word? Oh, You know Lord, You know! Your word is *living and active*! And if the feet of those who preach the *Gospel of peace* and good news are beautiful,[5] how much more beautiful is Your word? – For it is Your word that make such feet beautiful! In light of these truths, should I not be all the more diligent to grow in Your word? – Oh Yes! Lord, is it not in and through Your word, along with earnest prayer, that the beginning, and continuation, of walking You is formed? And not only the beginning and continuation, but also the preparation of being equipped to face many kinds of trials and especially that of fear? Oh how precious and beautiful is this hidden pathway to godliness and simplicity of faith, so light of burdens and filled with joy, such that words cannot give proof to the value.

Oh how true was the saying of the *Preacher*, "*The end of the matter; all has been heard. Fear God and keep His commandments, for this is the whole duty of man. For God will bring every deed into judgment, with every secret thing,*

---

[1] John 1:14

[2] Matthew 5:17

[3] James 1:13-15

[4] Hebrews 4:12

[5] Romans 10:15; Isaiah 52:7

whether good or evil."[1] For at the end of the day, meaning the basics of my life this moment, I cannot change yesterday – for I can only learn from my mistakes, failures and lax disregard of Your Scriptures; tomorrow has not yet come – so it is best not to fret and become consumed with the unknown; however, I have today! For today I can seek You, Your kingdom and Your righteousness,[2] being transformed by Your word and growing in the beautiful and greatest of all commandments.[3]

Lord, make me wise like the man who found great treasure[4] and the one who found a pearl of great value[5] - to sell all I have wrongly valued, even the good things I have esteemed more highly than I should, so that I would have all my treasure in You and Your inspired, sufficient and infallible word. Make me such a one, oh Lord, that desires eternally lasting things and that I am found diligent and resolved walking with You in reality, thus being prepared for the dark and difficult days to come. Search my heart Lord,[6] know me and prove whether these things are true in me. To Your glory, Your name and Your dear Son, may Your word be fanned into ever increasing flame, for You have *"not given me a spirit of fear but of power and love and self-control."*[7] Help me to understand and apply such lofty truths. Amen.

---

[1] Ecclesiastes 12:13, 14

[2] Matthew 6:33

[3] Matthew 22:35-40

[4] Matthew 13:44

[5] Matthew 13:45

[6] Psalm 139:23

[7] 2 Timothy 1:6, 7

"Feeding our minds with the word of Christ is essential if our hearts are to be filled with the joy of Christ. Yet, despite this, we are all too slow to read and meditate on the Scriptures, to seek to master them as far as we can, and in the process be mastered by them. There is no substitute here for dogged daily discipline. It is a battle to find the time; it can be a harder battle to fight sloth. But we need to overcome the habit of reading Scripture only when we 'feel like it'. For in one sense it is an 'acquired taste'. Only when we learn to read and meditate on it no matter what we feel like we will actually begin to feel like reading it. Scripture is medicine for our sick souls. The label says, 'Take daily' not 'Take when you feel like it'! If we do only the latter it is likely that we will never 'feel better'!"[1]

---

[1] Sinclair B. Ferguson, *Maturity: Growing Up and Going On in the Christian Life*, p. 49

Chapter Four

Preparing before the trials

"Stay dressed for action and keep your lamps burning, and be like men who are waiting for their master to come home from the wedding feast, so that they may open the door to him at once when he comes and knocks. Blessed are those servants whom the master finds awake when he comes."

Luke 12:35-37

Lord, here I find myself, I must admit, too often weak and distracted, taken up with the duties of the day and nearly swallowed by the routine in the mundane life, here in the midst of a culture of affluence and prosperity. Oh that I would remember how Sodom fell and that I would not be like their deeper heart condition – *"Behold, this was the guilt of your sister Sodom: she and her daughters had pride, excess of food, and prosperous ease, but did not aid the poor and needy."*[1] Even though I may let myself, however unintentional, drift towards mental slumber and wander into

---

[1] Ezekiel 16:49

the grounds of the self-life, You are continuously faithful to guide and direct my paths and alert me to my spiritual dryness. You, oh Lord, by Your providence have placed me in this time and in this culture, so should I complain against You? No, for I repent, turning unto You again this very day. And should I seek to escape this culture of corruption? On the one hand, I know it is far better to be absent from the body to be with You,[1] however, I know there is work here yet to do, regardless if it is labor and toiling, work and hardship, pain and problems, yet You have good and lasting promises and joyous good works for me yet here as well; not only this, but that someone by the words I speak or write may be humble tool that You would use to save their soul. May Your will be done.

Never let me forget that my fellowship is not with this world, that being with darkness and sin, but with You now and here, in reality and truth; for here I must be found praising Your name, living for You, being prepared and trained up for eternity and the many trials that will come my way. For until the last beat of my heart and last breath of my lungs, till the life You have given and sustained, is call back to You, here it is I must be about Your will. In this, Lord, may I be so *dressed for action*, and with increasing dedication and time being *shut-up* to You, and may I be burn bright with the light of Christ.

Lord, should I seek You only when I am in want of relief, or when desirous of some good thing, or to know of some sort of thing I am to do? And although, Lord, I am to seek You in

---

[1] 2 Corinthians 5:8; Philippians 1:23

these times as well, rather how much more should I seek You when the comforts of life and routine commonality are upon me? Oh that I might increase in self-discipline and resolve to be alert and ready at the door. Without doubt, and You know Lord, many of my days physical pain comes to befriend me and remind me of my temporal weaknesses; yet in this too You have taught me, and preparing me still further, to praise You in the trials,[1] for You only have my eternal best in mind.[2] For what Satan means for evil, You use for good.[3] May I dwell more on Your incredible goodness during trials, as I have so often in the past, more so soon (see chapter eight).

In this walk with You I am being prepared and made ready for many battles. You have shown me time and again that my focus is not to be on the battles, the trials, the enemy, nor even the overall war, but it is to be on and with You alone. Here, oh Lord, make me to be sober-minded and singular focused; only when I am walking with You, with full attention on You, am I able to understand how to put on the battle armor and how to use the weapons rightly.[4] For how can I be strong in You and in the power of Your might[5] if my attention is divided, or worse yet, wrongly locked upon things other than You? How can I be a right, true and maturing Christian if milk[6] is what I drink and the cares of this world is my appetite? Oh Lord – forbid such! For like newborn babies I

---

[1] James 1:2

[2] Romans 8:28, 29

[3] Genesis 50:20

[4] Ephesians 6:11

[5] Ephesians 6:10

[6] Hebrews 5:12; 1 Corinthians 3:2

must long for the *pure spiritual milk,*[1] however, I must only start with such longing – my longing must continue to grow and continue itself, to long for more and more of You. So help me, rather work in me Lord, a growing spiritual awareness and preparedness, *paying much closer attention*[2] to Your word and Your powerfully working Holy Spirit.

And is it not even more than just being prepared generally, should I not be in the school of piety and holiness as well? For without holiness, shall I even see You? NO![3] Yet this school is not laborious nor unwilling, it is also not a mere moral legalism nor imprisonment of my desires, but one of joyously learning how I ought to respond and act like Jesus at all times, especially when the fires of affliction, trials and fears are sure to test my profession. Herein, Lord, for the sake of Your great name, the sake of Your dear Son and Your blessed Holy Spirit, try me and know my heart, *lead me in the way everlasting.*[4]

Lord, today you remind me yet again that *to whom much was given, much will be required.*[5] So how could it be, as I have experienced in some of the years gone by, that I had ever become like some of those in the church in Ephesus?

---

[1] 1 Peter 2:2
[2] Hebrews 2:1
[3] Hebrews 12:14
[4] Psalm 139:23, 24
[5] Luke 12:48

"But I have this against you, that you have abandoned the love you had at first. Remember therefore from where you have fallen; repent, and do the works you did at first."[1]

Oh Lord, you know how I have been in such a place, but You, oh You mighty Lord, You awakened me to my state, my state of great need for You; of course not in mere words or *self-puffed-up* knowledge[2] condemning of sin, but authentically knowing You and rightly doing the good works You have prepared ahead for me; is this not what makes the reality of faith alone and my desire to respond by doing good works cheerfully related friends?[3] Certainly yes! For if You have given me so very much, as You have given me the greatest of all, thus namely Jesus Your Son, Your Christ, how then shall I respond to you? Shall I not desire to be awake, alert and ready at the helm? Should this not be more than mere preparation, should it not also be a working out of the salvation which You have granted me?[4] Still further yet, should this not cause me to fulfill the greatest of commissions, to live the greatest of commandments, to be built up in love and to build up my fellow man in Your powerful and working graces, even considering others greater than myself? Oh, and should I not be in prayer, prayer for those who are fellow laborers in the Gospel, those in need of regeneration, and yes, even authentically praying for those who hate me? Oh Lord, for if you have given me such grace, such pardon and favor, should I not but respond to You and let my actions show the

---

[1] Revelation 2:4, 5
[2] 1 Corinthians 8:1
[3] Ephesians 2:10
[4] Philippians 2:12

truth even when no one else can see it but You alone? Oh Lord, You know – Oh how You know!

So then, how can I express, how shall I comprehend, how shall I intercede for my dear brothers and sisters? Lord, help me to express how the longing of the church sounds; help me, dear Lord, to listen, to feel, to intercede for the suffering, and the very blood that cries out from the ground unto You.[1] And should I forget about those in bondage and prisons, those being abused and exploited by the evil one? Oh Lord, never, for You see and know such ones! Should not that which concerns You be not my concern as well? You see into places, places concealed in such a way as to appear good, living in the light, and even religiously pious, yet are dens of horrid evil. Take the priests in Ezekiel's day, they tried such things,[2] but You Lord know and reveal such wickedness. As a very cherished preacher once said to me, *"God uses rocks and donkeys to speak"*[3], Oh Lord, how much more ought I to cry out to You and to be a voice for the voiceless, especially in light of Your great mercy and love You have lavished upon me, You being the Greatest when I was the worst? Oh to cry out to You, to lift high the voiceless and make the case of the widow and fatherless known[4], and to verbalize for the persecuted and hidden soul; shall I not do as I am able, and even to call someone to their aide and make their reality felt?[5] Shall I not make intersession my life's response to what You

---

[1] Genesis 4:10

[2] Ezekiel 8:1-18

[3] Numbers 22:28-30; Luke 19:40

[4] Isaiah 1:17

[5] Hebrews 13:3

have given me and do as I am able? Lord work this out in me much, much more than I am even now aware.

Even in these things, Oh Lord, I feel Satan tempting me to twist Your graces into my prideful and personal usage and wicked presumptions[1] upon Your holy, good and perfect character. Lord, let me not, no never, do what is right in my own sight,[2] for there is no wisdom in my eyes, only in repentance will it be *healing to my flesh* and *refreshment to my bones*.[3] For You hate pride, arrogance, the evil path and perverted speech.[4] But oh what promises You have for me and all who will be so awake and ready, prepared and working – *"I love those who love Me, and those who seek Me diligently find Me."*[5]

So then since I have received so much, shall I not be like Enoch,[6] who having no Bible, no formulated church, no men's groups, nor fellowship with others that I know, shall I not walk with You all the more? For in knowing You is true insight,[7] fellowship[8] and friendship, closer than any human brother, sister, mother, father and although a symbol of Your church, even marriage.[9] You have not left me ignorant of

---

[1] Romans 2:4

[2] Judges 17:6, 21:25

[3] Proverbs 3:7, 8

[4] Proverbs 8:13

[5] Proverbs 8:17

[6] Genesis 5:22, 24

[7] Proverbs 9:10

[8] 1 John 1:3

[9] Ephesians 5:31, 32

Satan's devices[1] and I know all too well, that there is no man, nothing of the flesh, that can offer deep, lasting and true freedom, joy and peace. For You call me to hate even the garment stained by the flesh[2] and to turn away from trusting in the flesh – so why then would I, how could I dare give but an ounce of my time to the learning of enmities and vanities of death? Forbid this in me! *"Cursed is the man who trusts in man and makes flesh his strength."*[3]

How then shall I respond to You? How shall I forget to be diligent, not just merely laying hold of initial salvation, but really and deeply, passionately and rightly, in recognition and in humility, seek to know more and more and more, oh so ever increasing? Let me not be like Lot's wife, looking back and longing for sinful ease,[4] but let me be like the one who's hand is put to the plow, focused forward[5] and being trained by Your true[6] and working grace.[7] May the soils of my old man continually be plowed up and ready made fertile ground, always ready for Your word, the seeds of life – Christ Jesus Himself, and Your water, the growing and working of Your Holy Spirit, be ever increasingly productive till that great day. Be it ever so true. Amen.

---

[1] 2 Corinthians 2:11

[2] Jude 1:23

[3] Jeremiah 17:5-10

[4] Genesis 19:26

[5] Luke 9:62

[6] 1 Peter 5:12

[7] Titus 2:11-14

"How good is God thus to prepare me by sufferings, that so His blessings may not be my ruin. These things to the natural man are not joyous, but grievous; but God enables me to take comfort in Him, to thank Him sincerely for His loving correction, and therefore when I am sufficiently exercised thereby, I hope it will bring forth in me the peaceable fruits of righteousness. Amen."[1]

---

[1] George Whitefield, *George Whitefield Journals*, p. 169-70, Banner of Truth

Section Two

My Response in Trials

*"God is faithful, by whom you were called into the
fellowship of His Son, Jesus Christ our Lord."*

1 Corinthians 1:9

Chapter Five

Your Example

"For to this you have been called, because Christ also suffered for you, leaving you an example, so that you might follow in his steps."

1 Peter 2:21

Lord, tonight I cannot but help to think of how You are a strong and might tower,[1] and yet just how weak and fragile I really am; help me Lord to run to You for I know that in my way and in my eyes, I am too often blinded; so weigh me, show me how to commit my work unto You.[2] I do not want to merely have some 'sense', or 'feeling' for which way seems right, for surely if left to myself, the end of this way is death.[3] Oh Lord, teach me Your statutes[4] and paths, and may Your truths, Your will, Your incredible attributes be stamped forever in my mind. I must here ask, am I sincere and

---

[1] Proverbs 18:10
[2] Proverbs 16:2, 3
[3] Proverbs 16:25
[4] Psalm 119:12

true in my devotion and relation to You? Do I really seek to be conformed and comforted, with increasing fervor, by and through Your word? Shall I heed the beautifully narrow, yet oftentimes difficult and at times humanly lonely, paths of Christ? Shall I conform my life to Your will, especially when trials come and tarry for an extended season? If I shall say yes, then because Christ suffered for me, shall I not walk out in His footsteps? Oh Lord, by Your Spirit shall I do so; convict me[1] and teach me this path and let my eyes be transfixed upon Christ as He was no stranger to the trials, the temptations and the fears as well.[2]

"Have this mind among yourselves, which is yours in Christ Jesus, who, though He as in the form of God, did not count equality with God a thing to be grasped, but emptied Himself, by taking the form of a servant, being born in the likeness of men. And being found in human form, He humbled Himself by becoming obedient to the point of death, even death on a cross."[3]

Is it not better for me that I should *suffer for doing good, if that should be* Your *will, than for doing evil?*[4] Most certainly! However, I must admit Lord, knowing this when in study or when the throes of many trials seem but far away, is a simple thing, one I find, left too quickly in thought and rarely transmitted to application and praise. When the trials, fears, doubts, or even anger they come, Jesus should be the very first

---

[1] John 16:8
[2] Hebrews 4:15
[3] Philippians 2:5-8
[4] 1 Peter 3:17

and final focus of my eyes; however, I must admit that this is not always what I first do. Lord, cause me to turn to you in the good and the difficult and dangerous seasons that I might praise You, seek You and listen to Your Spirit as the very first of my responses. Oh Lord, keep sin, evil and temptations far from me,[1] especially here where people look to see if I should fall, and then to accuse You of not being real. Oh for Your great name, build me into such a person who dwells with You and is ever learning from Your word.

And yet, how shall I respond to the trials I face today? Is not Satan, that devil of old,[2] seeming to work overtime today? So how and what shall be my response this day? Shall I cower and retreat, shall I make a claim to grace and yet live in sin,[3] shall I only be in prayer and do nothing? No. I must respond according to Your will. These times, although looking darker moment by moment, are not nearly as dark as the hearts of men really are[4] in comparison to You and Your holiness. All of these things are of no surprise to You, for You alone are sovereign and all together omniscient, there is no new sin under heaven.[5]

Oh praise be unto You, for You have not left me an orphan[6] nor unaware,[7] but You have left me Your will, Your way, the very example of Your dear Son; more amazingly yet, as if that

---

[1] Matthew 6:13

[2] Revelation 20:2

[3] Romans 6:1, 15

[4] Genesis 6:5, 8:21

[5] Ecclesiastes 1:9

[6] John 14:18

[7] 2 Corinthians 2:11 – more in chapter ten

were not enough to praise You already, He (Jesus) calls me His brother.[1] How could such amazing grace be granted me? Lord, may a great many people come to know such grace, such mercies, such incredible love – may they experience and grow in You, not in the things of this world, but in You – for You alone are immutable.

Lord, cause me to learn from Your word, trust in Your word and live by the rule of Your word, especially during the preparation and execution of the fiery trials that come.

> *"He committed no sin, neither was deceit found in His mouth. When he was reviled, He did not revile in return, when He suffered, He did not threaten, but continued entrusting Himself to Him who judges justly."*[2]

Lord, so much learning is found here, so much conviction and so much pure spiritual gold. It is amazing to think that Jesus left such an example; it seems so impossible, and indeed it truly is apart from You and the *washing of regeneration and renewal of the Holy Spirit.*[3] For Lord, You, by Your *divine power, has granted to* me *all things that pertain to life and godliness,*[4] so never let me become *so nearsighted that I am blind, having forgotten.*[5] So may these words above be in me and remind me when in trials to follow the example of the Lord Jesus when He suffered.

---

[1] Hebrews 2:11

[2] 1 Peter 2:22, 23

[3] Titus 3:5

[4] 2 Peter 1:3

[5] 2 Peter 1:8, 9

1.) He committed no sin

2.) There was no deceit found in His mouth

3.) When He was criticized with bitterness, heavy anger and direct enmity, He did not act such in return

4.) When He suffered, He did not return threats – furthermore, He responded…

5.) …by continuing to entrust Himself to You. Lord, help me to develop this as my response in the midst of trials.

I am reminded of what the Apostle Paul said, *"For the sake of Christ, then, I am content with weaknesses, insults, hardships, persecutions, and calamities. For when I am weak, then I am strong."*[1] How content am I Lord, for Christ's sake, when I am in trials that are lesser than these? Forgive me when I complain and grumble[2] when such things are common to the true Christian.[3] Over the years, Lord, You have been teaching me to consider it all joy[4] and to authentically praise you while patiently enduring[5] the valleys of this life. I still remember the first time I was given greater grace to praise You during a time of a burdening trial – Oh such a sweet fellowship and tremendous joy You bestowed upon me. Forgive me for not always prevailing and learning from that experience, forgive me for not always trusting You in my

---

[1] 1 Corinthians 12:10
[2] Philippians 2:14
[3] 2 Timothy 3:12
[4] James 1:2 – more in chapter eight
[5] James 1:12

trials. Oh but You, yes You oh Lord, even when my heart condemns me, You are greater than my heart![1] Would it not be better to experience sovereignly placed thorns in the flesh, that I might be able to have a greater revelation of You, of Your grace, and of Your power?[2] Oh yes! For these thorns are designed to humble me and break the pride and conceit, so shall I not praise You? Most certainly, however, You know just how much grace I need, Your grace and Your power is what I need to see clearly, be alert and understanding my need to praise You in the trials. Lord, grow me here!

For if I seek to escape the trials and the appointed thorns, am I not saying that I know what is best for me? Am I not saying that I desire for the lesser things of this life and ease of the flesh? Cause me to say and earnestly mean,

"But I do not account my life of any value nor as precious to myself, if only I may finish my course and the ministry that I received from the Lord Jesus, to testify to the gospel of the grace of God."[3]

Regardless of what comes my way, whether sleeplessness, a burdened mind, physical pains that tarry, or more like my blessed brothers and sisters who currently (and past generations) suffer so greatly, may I be found to say, *"I do not account my life of any value..."* Strengthen, oh Lord, my brothers and sisters who...

---

[1] 1 John 3:20
[2] 2 Corinthians 12:7-9
[3] Acts 20:24

"Some were tortured, <u>refusing to accept release, so that they might rise again to a better life</u>. Others suffered mocking and flogging, and even chains and imprisonment. They were stoned, they were sawn in two, they were killed with the sword. They went about in skins of sheep and goats, destitute, afflicted, mistreated – of whom the world was not worthy – wandering about in deserts and mountains, and in dens and caves of the earth."[1]

Help me to remember, that You are always in full control and that there is no place where I can escape from You.[2] For even when Jesus was on the cross and cried out, *"Eli, Ele, lema sabachthani?"*[3] – was He not quoting, thus proving Himself, in full-control? Oh Yes! He suffered and fulfilled everything according to Your inspired, all-sufficient, infallible and immutable word – He was the very word.[4] He was the *crushed worm* of Psalm twenty-two, He walked through the *valley of the shadow of death* of Psalm twenty-three and He commanded that *the gates and ancient doors be lifted up* that He, the King of glory, would enter. Since You are in such control, how can I not trust You in and with my trials? Shall I not let you be the victor and hero of my life? Or shall I look to myself, casting You aside, by trusting in my own strength? Would it not be better to see Your strong arm prove Yourself? Absolutely, yes and amen. So then, Lord, teach me to get out of Your way and to look to Jesus and the example left for me.

---

[1] Hebrews 11:35b-38

[2] Psalm 139:7-13

[3] Matthew 27:46; Mark 15:34

[4] John 1:14

"Set a guard, O Lord, over my mouth; keep watch over the door of my lips! Do not let my heart incline to any evil, to busy myself with wicked deeds in company with men who work iniquity, and let me not eat of their delicacies!"[1]

Although I face many types of distractions and temptations, trials and fears, and a culture of sin, death and a world of sissified grace, may I be a man who is truly seeking to walk with you always more closely. May Your strong hand be revealed to me, in me and through me that I would see You always as my greatest of treasures and most precious of all things. May I become more aware and alert to Your nearness, like the preacher of old Thomas Chalmers used to preach, that the *expulsive power of Your new affection* would remove all idols and old affections.[2]

---

[1] Psalms 141:3, 4
[2] See Thomas Chalmers, *The Expulsive Power of a New Affection*

"So that night I said, 'Lord Jesus show me the truth of what happened that day.' I opened my kindle up to the Bible and I put my finger and it said, 'Vengeance is mine says the Lord, I will repay.'

"Vengeance, oh, what I thought was justice was vengeance. Vengeance looks like justice but is driven by hate. It starts in the same place – an injustice has been done – what you going to do about it? To get justice requires you to approach that unjust act with love for the perpetrator and the person whose hurt – and mercy – there's a place for punishment too, and enforcement – but it will be done in the spirit of love, which is very different. What's the best for both these people?

"And I said, 'Jesus forgive me. And I reject vengeance.' And He took it away from me. And it was a huge crushing weight on me, but I could not feel it until it was lifted off."[1]

---

[1] David Eubank, Missionary and Free Burma Rangers Founder, *Free Burma Rangers Movie*

Chapter Six

Armcd by You

*"Since therefore Christ suffered in the flesh, arm yourselves
with the same way of thinking..."*

1 Peter 4:1

Father, I thank you this day as you have yet again reminded me, although my heart is deceptive and cannot in itself be trusted,[1] yet You can and do often right my emotions; and how is it I know if my emotions and desires of my heart are right, are of You, do they not conform and agree with Your word, Your will and in the truth. I praise You for the Holy Spirit, His guidance and correction, His confirmation and witness[2] in my life. Oh, You know Father just how frail I am and how I need Your encouragement and hope. Cause me Lord, develop and strengthen me, that I might increase in strides, that I might *arm myself with the same way of thinking.* Since *Christ suffered for me in the flesh,* may *I full up in* the

---

[1] Jeremiah 17:9
[2] Romans 8:16

sufferings[1] of the flesh, denying myself, picking up my cross and following after You.[2] May I come to see this, much deeper and truer yet, that this is a joyous place in You to be found, and not because any works or sufferings of mine could ever earn me salvation, but that my response in trials would be to think like Jesus.

Shall I not set my sights *so as to live for the rest of the time in the flesh no longer for human passions but for Your will?*[3] And what is Your will for me in this? Is this not love? Oh most certainly yes! And yet in this area I need to grow so much more. Your will regarding the context of this mindset, regarding suffering, thus starts here –

"Therefore let those who suffer according to God's will entrust their souls to a faithful creator while doing good."[4]

It is indeed good for me that I recognize that any suffering I experience is already known by You, and in recognition of this light, I must respond by entrusting myself to You, the faithful creator. Am I about the doing of good during such times, and at all times? And should I be surprised when fiery trials come? No, for such is the testing[5] and promises for those who have even a desire to be godly in Christ.[6]

---

[1] Colossians 1:24

[2] Matthew 10:38, 16:24; Mark 8:34; Luke 9:23, 14:27

[3] 1 Peter 4:2

[4] 1 Peter 4:19

[5] 1 Peter 4:12

[6] 2 Timothy 3:12; Philippians 1:29; also see: Matthew 10:22-25, 13:21, 24:9; Luke 6:22, 21:12-19; John 15:18-23

Lord, here I feel I must thank You yet again, for You have reminded me that context regarding Your word matters a great deal. I should never use Your word to justify my sin, nor use it to avoid suffering, nor even use a part of it to attempt to nullify another part where I am lacking in understanding. No never let this be of me.

Now having these things before me, I want to be reminded, over and over if that is where I am in need, to Your truths, promises and commands found prior to the words, *"Since therefore"*, as found in 1st Peter 4:1 and the surrounding context down to 1st Peter 4:19. May I see the further necessity of doing good and entrusting You in these passages; help me, encourage me and cause my response during trials to be that which honors and glorifies You.

A prior review (1 Peter 4:1) for a mindset on Christ, Your promises and my edification in responding rightly.

I.   Jesus suffered for me that He would bring me to You. – 1 Peter 3:18 (John 17:3)

II.   If I am jealous for what is good, who can harm me? – 1 Peter 3:13 (Matthew 10:28; Luke 12:5)

III.   a.) honor Christ the Lord as holy; b.) to always be prepared to make a defense for the hope that is in me; c.) do this with gentleness, respect and with a good conscience. –1 Peter 3:15-17

IV.   a.) I must have unity of mind, sympathy, brotherly love, a tender heart, and a humble mind; b.) not repaying evil or reviling, but bless others – 1 Peter 3:8, 9

V.	Even in the privacy and intimacy of marriage, and context of submission to God, and suffering, my conduct must be radically opposite of this world – and for my prayers not to be hindered. – 1 Peter 3:7

A surrounding review (1 Peter 4:1-19) for the good works I may be doing in the midst of suffering and trials.

I.	To live for the will of God. – vs. 4:2
II.	To put away foolishness and lawlessness. – vs. 4:3-6
III.	To know that the end of all things is at hand – the start of the end of days and the beginning of the labor pains. And yet, my response needs to be according to Your word, self-controlled, sober-minded, again, for the sake of my prayers. – vs. 4:7
IV.	Above all, I must keep loving one another – vs. 4:8
V.	Show hospitality without grumbling – vs. 4:9
VI.	Use the gifts to serve one another, being a good steward of Your varied grace. – vs. 4:10
VII.	In everything – You may be glorified through Your dear Son. – vs. 4:11
VIII.	Rejoice insofar as I share Christ's sufferings – Why? That I may also rejoice and be glad when Christ's glory is revealed. – vs. 4:13
IX.	If I am insulted for the name of Christ, I am blessed – How? …because the Spirit of glory and You rest upon me. – vs. 4:14
X.	Do not suffer as an evil doer. – vs. 4:15
XI.	Be not ashamed if I suffer as a Christian, but rather glorify You and in Your name. – vs. 4:16
XII.	*"For it is time for judgment to begin at the household of God; and if it begins with us, what will*

*be the outcome for those who do not obey the Gospel
of God? And, 'If the righteous is scarcely saved,
what will become of the ungodly and the sinner?'" –*
vs. 4:17, 18

Lord, I praise You for Your word and right viewpoint for how I ought to respond and act as a true Christian, and this in response to Your *true grace*.[1] I see so many areas, even after these last two decades, I am still so lacking in my obedience and conformity to Christ. Make these passages sink deep in my soul and may they pave the way unto good works and a right mindset, especially amid the trials and valleys.

And yet, to have Your will and this way of arming my mind to think, shall it not require devoted time in the word and before Your throne? Shall it not require me being transformed by the renewal of the mind,[2] not in ways of this world, but through Your word? Does it not mean I must be mulled over so that I may be tested, tested that I may discern what is Your good, acceptable and perfect will? And does it not require greater amounts of Your grace? And does this grace not come from You? To all the above – YES. And will You deny me any good thing according to Your will shall I ask? No. Then shall I not ask for more of You, and to have You as the primary interest of my life? And although there is a great amount of practicality that is applicable to doing Your work, responding to my trials and my proper daily reactions and interactions, how can I know the truth? and respond in truth if I am lax to walk in the truth? For whatever do I have to

---

[1] 1 Peter 5:12
[2] Romans 12:2

offer anyone in way of lasting eternal help and hope, truth and power, if You are not powerfully working in me a life of sanctification and humility? For Your kingdom does not consist in word, but in power.[1] You are able to do far more abundantly than all I could ask or think.[2]

Lord, in the midst of all the evil and straight up demonic activity of this current day, and all that the enemy has purposed to do against You and against Your church, I ask that You would make me to be a man after Your own heart, a man holy and set apart to mature in You. Like Jeremiah, who was surrounded by enemies and false witnesses, cause me to be like him when he says,

"If I say, 'I will not mention Him, or speak any more in His name,' there is in my heart as it were a burning fire shut up in my bones, and I am weary with holding it in, and I cannot."[3]

And make me to be like Micah, who was also surrounded by enemies, feeling undone and gleaned, and unable to trust anyone, said,

"But as for me, I will look to the Lord; I will wait for the God of my salvation; my God will hear me."[4]

Oh what resolve, what fortitude of Your Holy Spirit in such men. Oh Lord, make this to be the continual increase of my life, and to be marked by deep permanent love, to increase in

---

[1] 1 Corinthians 4:20
[2] Ephesians 3:20
[3] Jeremiah 20:9
[4] Micah 7:7

loving You and my fellow man – for this is the type of arming of the mind that I need so much the more.

"Not a step can the believer advance without the Spirit. Not a victory can he achieve without the Spirit. Not a moment can he exist without the Spirit. As he needed him at the first, so he needs him all his journey through."[1]

"Where are the young men and women of this generation who will hold their lives cheap, and be faithful even unto death, who will lose their lives for Christ's, flinging them away for love of him? Where are those who will live dangerously, and be reckless in this service? Where are the men of prayer? Where are the men who count God's Word of more importance to them than their daily food? Where are the men who, like Moses of old, commune with God face to face as a man speaks with his friend? Where are God's men in this day of God's power?"[2]

---

[1] Octavius Winslow, *The Work of the Holy Spirit*, p. 22
[2] Howard Guinness, *Sacrifice*

Chapter Seven

To be emptied

"Have this mind among yourselves, which is yours in Christ Jesus, who though He was in the form of God, did not count equality with God a thing to be grasped, but emptied Himself, by taking the form of a servant..."

Philippians 2:5-7a

Today, oh Lord, I cannot but help to feel my heart dull and distracted by so many secondary and lesser things, things of no eternal value. It seems such a battle this day – Oh Lord – help me this day to *have this mind* for myself, which is mine, in Christ Jesus, that I would be emptied of my selfish desires and in living for the flesh, *but in humility* I would *count others more significant than myself.*[1] And does this not begin, continue and grow in intercessory prayer for the souls and needs of others? Oh yes! Make this the focus of my private life, one authentic, deep and true unto You. Although the trials they be many, is this not the very first lesson in my

---

[1] Philippians 2:4

trials, that being conformity to Christ (being emptied) and good works (that for others above self)?

How then shall I come to You this day? Shall I not set my mind to praise You and seeking greater measures of You, regardless of my feelings, and then to pray for my fellow believers, family, friends, and especially those who are being terribly abused and unable to defend themselves? Should I not intercede for the children being used and tortured by pure evil? Oh Lord God, Oh Lord, how You know! Oh God, come and destroy this evil, destroy this wickedness that is so far deeper than most could ever perceive; even should some have a sort of outright knowledge of this wickedness, it still is one hundred thousand times worse in Your eyes and omniscience.

And here too I find, like so many, the distracting temptation to think and ask wrongly of Your character and actions. There are so many who want to know: *"How could a good and loving God allow such wickedness to continue?"* However, this is not only the wrong question, but You have made this but so very plain in Your word.[1] The problem with mankind and myself, of course resulting of the sinful fall, is that we refuse to ask the greater question and believe what You have already said. The question I must never forget, that being far greater that the former, is this: *"How is it that I, a vile wretch whose best works are nothing more than a dirty rag,[2] should see any good, any love, any grace, any mercy from You God?"* And does not Your word clearly state, over and over again,

---

[1] Consider (for starters): Romans 3:3, 5:8, 9:22; Revelation 15:1-4; Acts 2:22, 23, 4:27, 28; Job chapters 38-41

[2] Isaiah 64:6

and also testified by Your Holy Spirit to my spirit, that I am far worse off, far more wicked, far more wretched and far more sin natured than I can even comprehend? Oh Yes! The question above always is a great help which causes me to respond to You in genuine humility[1] and with a broken and contrite heart.[2]

Lord, today in this dullness of mine, help me to pray and help me to sense the deep need now. How true it is and how thankful I am:

"…the Spirit helps us in our weakness. For we do not know what to pray for as we ought, but the Spirit Himself intercedes for us with groanings too deep for words. And He who searches hearts knows what is the mind of the Spirit, because the Spirit intercedes for the saints according to the will of God."[3]

Praise You my God, for not only does Your Spirit intercede for me according to Your will, so does Your dear precious Son.[4] And what amazing promises You have given to me, that even when I feel so in adequate in prayer, and unknowing of how or what to pray, or even simply undesiring, You even give Your grace to help me here. Further yet, You promise:

"Who shall separate us from the love of Christ? Shall tribulation, or distress, or persecution, or famine, or nakedness, or danger or sword? As it is written, 'For your

---

[1] James 4:10

[2] Psalm 51:17

[3] Romans 8:26, 27

[4] Romans 8:34

sake we are being killed all the day long; we are regarded as sheep to be slaughtered.' No in all these things we are more than conquerors through Him who loved us. For I am sure that neither death nor life, nor angels nor rulers, nor things present nor things to come, nor powers, nor height nor depth, nor anything else in all creation, will be able to separate us from the love of God in Christ Jesus our Lord."[1]

If Your love be so binding and Your strength so powerful and mighty, then what shall I fear when the trials come? Oh shall I not praise You for the affliction which purifies my soul? More than that, but the afflictions that ought to cause me to be *"broken bread and poured out wine"*[2] for the sake of others.

Having been reminded of these truths again today, Lord, I desire to authentically say, and even more so to be deeply marked in truth, by what the Apostle Paul said:

"For I consider that the sufferings of this present time are not worth comparing with the glory that is to be revealed to us."[3]

For how true it is that if I am to be a legitimate child of Yours, shall I not also *suffer with Him in order that I may also be glorified with Him*?[4] Lord let me not ask the easy and soft questions, rather deepen a resolve in me to put away the mindset of ease and of easy offenses. For when I think of the

---

[1] Romans 8:35-39
[2] Oswald Chambers, *My Utmost For His Highest*
[3] Romans 8:18
[4] Romans 8:17

true church over history, the disciples, early Anabaptists, Scottish Covenanters, Presbyterians, and many more, and how greatly they suffered, I must ask myself if I am willing to go to such the same places. When I think about the believers today being raped, tortured and mangled for the faith – that in trusting, in resting and in following Christ's path – I cannot help but to ask Your forgiveness for complaining against and running too soon away from such lesser trials. Forgive me, Lord, when I act and respond so wrongly and contrary to Your will. And although they are still trials, regardless of severity, let me take it deadly serious that I submit to Your strong and everlasting arm, for the arm of my flesh and my strength pales in comparison, and in all reality is not a comparison to You at all!

The problem so often with me is that I think too highly of my own strength, my own abilities and my own wisdom,[1] then what comes? Is it not my downfall, failure and sin? And why would I not fall, for pride is opposed to humility, and without humility I am against You and in opposition to Your grace.[2] For *"the wise will merit honor, but fools get disgrace."*[3]Lord, how foolish it is of me to entertain any thoughts where I think I can war *"against the rulers, against the authorities, against the cosmic powers over this present darkness, against the spiritual forces of evil in the heavenly places"* when I am not prepared to *take up* the *sword of the Spirit.* If I am not reading

---

[1] Proverbs 16:18; Romans 12:3
[2] Proverbs 3:34; James 4:6; 1 Peter 5:5
[3] Proverbs 3:35

and studying, nor praying and pondering, nor applying the wisdom of Your word, I have not a weapon to wield.

And if my heart should say to me, "*Oh son, take it easy, do not fret, the Lord knows that you believe His word. It's ok that you hardly ever read or study it; for after all, you don't understand it all too well anyway and its not nearly as entertaining as television, technology, media or even some other book, so relax. He knows you mean well and have faith, so fret not that your Bible sits mostly closed.*" Oh what cursed thoughts of the evil one! What dark thoughts of my old nature! Oh Lord, crucify these! For to be without Your word is surly to be defenseless, defeated and in much darkness.

Lord, shall I not be emptied, and shown to be empty, in order that You would fill me?[1] You gave me a new heart,[2] and this for Your namesake, for You have written the law on my heart and remembered my sins no more.[3] I remember the very moment that Your powerful saving grace flooded my life and how using a dear brother and pastor, You confronted me with Your word; for you had to show me what would be my eternal end should I continue living as I was.[4] Not only this, what damage I was doing to that soon to be daughter of Yours as well. Praise You for Your convicting and lifegiving Spirit! Oh, how the praises of my mouth are so far inadequate and so far short of the worship and praise You deserve! You showed

---

[1] Ephesians 5:18
[2] Ezekiel 36:26
[3] Jeremiah 31:31-34
[4] 1 Corinthians 6:9-10

me that my works, my very best religious works[1] (not that I had any) were of absolutely no help in the rescuing and resuscitation of my dead heart. For truly, it was *not by might, nor by power, but by Your Spirit*[2] that I was brought to awakening, repentance and faith in Your dear Son, Christ Jesus my Lord and Savior. Praise You almighty God!

And is this not how the path of my Lord was laid before me? Although He came to earth sinless and lived sinless,[3] yet He paved the path of suffering[4] trials and temptations,[5] was cruelly treated, bore the wrath for my sin *I deserved* and poured out His precious blood upon the tree.[6] If He was afflicted and mistreated, should I not embrace the same? For truly the suffering is nothing close to comparing with the precious glories of Christ. What is there in my past that compares to the joys, preciousness and experiential new heart of Christ's redemption and justification? Nothing can even begin to tip the scales in comparison to Your love! For it was Your will to crush[7] Your Son, on my behalf. Oh, what sacrificial love! He was the fulfillment of the Law and the prophets,[8] so He was, and is, the only One who could become the propitiation for my sins.[9] Oh what grace, mercy and great love, amazing love that laid down His life and satisfied Your

---

[1] Isaiah 64:6; Ephesians 2:8, 9

[2] Zechariah 4:6

[3] 1 Peter 1:19

[4] Hebrews 2:9; 1 Peter 3:18

[5] Hebrews 4:15

[6] Isaiah 53:5; Luke 24:46, 47

[7] Isaiah 53:10

[8] Matthew 5:17

[9] 1 John 2:2

justice and wrath against my sin. Never, never, never let me forget that I was brought up from the *dung heap*,[1] lost and wayward, and yet the *bruised reed You will not break and a smoldering wick You will not extinguish*,[2] so what boasting can I have in myself? None, no, never! And never let me forget that I must love as You have loved me, that I may be quick to give grace and offer up mercy to the one who comes down my path.

Should not these things be what stamp the mindset, the preparation, the being '*shut-up*' unto God, and when the trials of this life seem to be all too much? And should my trials get worse, should it be that I see days as dark as Habakkuk, shall I not respond to Your reality:

> *"But the Lord is in His holy temple; let all the earth keep silence before Him."*[3]

Will I respond to You waiting quietly[4] and will I rejoice in You and take joy?[5] Will You be my strength?[6] And if I personally should experience the wicked persecution and violent personal attacks like that of Alan Cameron, how shall I respond?

> *"Before the hangman set head and hands on the bloodstained Netherbow Port, the fingers pointing grimly*

---

[1] Psalm 113:7
[2] Isaiah 42:3; Matthew 12:20
[3] Habakkuk 2:20
[4] Habakkuk 3:16
[5] Habakkuk 3:18
[6] Habakkuk 3:19

upwards on either side of the head, a hero saint laying in prison was shown them. He was Alan Cameron, Covenanter. The cruel question was asked him. 'Do you know them?' His son's head and hands were very fair, being a man of fair complexion like himself. He kissed them saying, 'I know them, I know them. They are my son's, my own dear son's. <u>It is the Lord. Good is the will of the Lord, who cannot wrong me nor mine, but has made goodness and mercy to follow us all our days.</u>' A prisoner, head of a broken home, the father of martyred sons and daughter! It is the answer of the more-than-conqueror, the sufferer in Christ, full of faith and of the Holy Ghost; and having the heart full of the power and music of the Good Shepherd Psalm: 'Goodness and mercy all my life shall surely follow me; and in God's house for evermore my dwelling place shall be.'"[1]

Oh Lord, You know what kind of strength, power and humility You would cloth me with on such a day should Your will be the same for me. I never want to be like those who *shrink back,*[2] nor of those who endures for a while, and when tribulation or persecution arises on account of the word, immediately falls.[3] Should I not be so prepared in walking with You now? Should I not continue to be transformed and conformed in humility, with a mindset to be emptied of myself? Oh Yes! However, let this not be in some deceiving legalism or moralistic mindset that enslaves, rather would it be powerfully real and in devoted worship and in genuine

---

[1] Jock Purves, *Fair Sunshine: Character Studies of the Scottish Covenanters*, p. 37, 38, underline mine
[2] Hebrews 10:39
[3] Matthew 13:21

service and abiding sacrificial love. Oh, that reality and resolve would find their home here.

"When God intends to fill a soul, He first makes it empty; when He intends to enrich a soul, He first makes it poor; when He intends to exalt a soul, He first makes it humble; when He intends to save a soul, He first makes it sensible of its own miseries and nothingness."[1]

---

[1] John Flavel

Chapter Eight

Trusting and rejoicing

"And we know that for those who love God all things work together for good, for those who are called according to His purpose."

Romans 8:28

Oh mighty God, today I am so overwhelmed by Your goodness to me, yet again, what words shall I offer up to You? What thoughts can compare with You? Yet, oh God, do not all good and wise thoughts, thoughts concerning You, Your dear Son and Your blessed Holy Spirit, do they not come from You and Your inspired word? Oh praise You – Yes! And yet, even though vessels of mere dirt and clay, men and women who You have chosen to be Your people, blood brought and redeemed, do You not also use us to deliver the words of hope, life and encouragement, the very Gospel of truth? And again, to me this day You have so blessed me and encouraged me, enriched my inner being. Oh Lord, increase my love, my desire, my contentment, yes even my resolve for You; be my thoughts, my boast and my life this day, even more so than yesterday past.

There are so many exacting places and parts in my life that You have been working and transforming, destroying and building, yes making altogether new, yet in this area of knowing your eternal good for me, has this not been one of the greatest blessings in my life? Oh, You alone certainly know! Although, You know that I am only a babe in such graces, grow my trust and confidence in You, and that I might praise You continually through my trials.

And yet I have been blessed, not because of trials and difficulties, pains and thorns, have ceased to come, rather when they now come I am reminded of You, Your love, your grace, Your mercies; I am reminded of the Lord Jesus, His sufferings, His victory; I am reminded Your dear Son, the preeminent Christ. You have opened my eyes to see eternal realities and truths in that You *work all things*, even the things meant for evil against me, to be made useful for my eternal *good*. And this eternal good, is it not the conformity to the image of Your Son? Without a doubt – yes![1] For it is You who has called me and shown me grace; it is You who has justified[2] me and declared me innocent; it is You who redeemed my life;[3] it is You who first loved me;[4] it is You who will not let me go;[5] it is You who will glorify me.

---

[1] Romans 8:29

[2] Romans 8:30

[3] Romans 3:24

[4] 1 John 4:19

[5] John 10:28, 29

For all of this, shall I not respond to You? Shall I not search You out, seeking You as the most precious of all to behold? For all this, I have been given eyes of grace to see the eternal good You are working in and through me, even in the midst of trials and great difficulties.

"What then shall we say to these things? If God is for us, who can be against us?"[1]

And should greater and greater difficulties and pressures of refining fire come, oh that I should be able to look at all Your great faithfulness, Your great mercies, the greatness of You Yourself, and I hope to be like the three saints of old who where thrown into that blazing fire, I hope to be able to say like them:

"But if you do not worship, you shall immediately be cast into a burning fiery furnace. And who is the god who will deliver you out of my hands?'

"Shadrach, Meshach, and Abednego answered and said to the king, 'O Nebuchadnezzar, we have no need to answer you in this matter. If this be so, our God whom we serve is able to deliver us from the burning fiery furnace, and He will deliver us out of your hand, O king. But if not, be it known to you, O king, that we will not serve you gods or worship the golden image that you have set up.'"[2]

I too hope that this would be my reply, my resolve and my willingness, and I know that I can trust You now and then

---

[1] Romans 8:31
[2] Daniel 3:15-18

should such come according to Your will. Although my story may not be the same, I know I will too dance with *The Forth*,[1] Your dear Son, most precious and blessed Lord Jesus. I am so filled with thanksgiving for all of this. You have been teaching and training me to hear clearly Your voice and to follow You,[2] trusting and resting in You, and growing a desire to joyfully work for You.

Now herein, because of knowing that You work all things for my eternal good, for even Your discipline of me is because of Your unfailing love,[3] what joy and working grace You have bestowed upon me, I know that I am still often *"prone to wander, prone to leave the One I love."*[4] And although there are times where I am able to truly praise You, to *"count it all joy"* when the *"various kinds"* of trials come and test my faith,[5] I still find that often I must repent when my very first response is not to praise You. However, when this happens You have always been faithful to guide me back to Yourself, forgiving me yet again, and reminding me that You only work for my eternal good. For it is You alone which gives me such strength, such grace and such deep joy, and closeness with You, when I offer back to You what You have given me. Oh, how beautiful Your word does encourage me forward on this path:

---

[1] Daniel 3:25

[2] John 10:5, 27

[3] Hebrews 12:3-11

[4] *Come Thou Fount of Every Blessing*, Hymn

[5] James 1:2

"So Jesus also suffered outside the gate in order to sanctify the people through His own blood. Therefore let us go to Him outside the camp and bear the reproach He endured. For here we have no lasting city, but we seek the city that is to come. Through Him then let us offer up a sacrifice of praise to God, that is, the fruit of lips that acknowledge His name. Do not neglect to do good and to share what you have, for such sacrifices are pleasing to God."[1]

Shall not then my humble cry be like John the Baptist, *"He must increase, but I must decrease."*[2] Oh that I might also be willing to go *outside the camp* and offer up the *sacrifice of praise*; thus to be engaging my faith in trusting and rejoicing because You are so worthy. Shall I not say, although I have not yet experienced to the same degree, as the Apostle Paul:

"Indeed, I count everything as loss because of the surpassing worth of knowing Christ Jesus my Lord. For His sake I have suffered the loss of all things and count them as rubbish, in order that I may gain Christ and be found in Him, not having a righteousness of my own that comes from the law, but that which comes through faith in Christ, the righteousness from God that depends on faith – that I may know Him and the power of His resurrection, and my share in His sufferings, becoming like Him in His death, that by any means possible I may attain the resurrection from the dead."[3]

---

[1] Hebrews 13:12-16
[2] John 3:30
[3] Philippians 3:8-11

Oh, how magnificent is this word; how beautiful and propelling; how can I not offer up praises unto You in the trials of purification, especially my trials which are less costly than Paul's? Oh Lord, make me to be humble and contrite, seeking and longing and striving to follow the pathway of Christ. Lord, cause me to see clearly and follow Jesus as He prayed at Gethsemane[1] the night before His sacrifice of love and grace upon the cross for me. Oh how He must have prayed so truly, so fully so powerful and real, so alone with You. Let me learn and not fall asleep when the darkest hour approaches, but let me be more at the ready, ready to praise You when the times they seem the most difficult. Like one dear brother has said, *"Habakkuk moved from petition to praise."*[2]

"I hear, and my body trembles; my lips quiver at the sound; rottenness enters into my bones; my legs tremble beneath me. Yet I will quietly wait for the day of trouble to come upon people who invade us.

"Though the fig tree should not blossom, nor fruit be on the vines, the produce of the olive fail and the fields yield no food, the flock be cut off from the fold and there be no herd in the stalls, yet I will rejoice in the Lord; I will take joy in the God of my salvation.

"God, the Lord, is my strength; He makes my feet like the deer's; He makes me tread on high places."[3]

---

[1] Matthew 26:36-46
[2] Brian Long, Itinerant Preacher
[3] Habakkuk 3:16-19

"How slow we are to learn that God is willing to go to any lengths to transform us. No matter what it costs he has set his heart on us. The cross proves his determination. He means to make us like his Son, Jesus Christ. For this is the goal of our maturity. It should not surprise us that this is an arduous process. We require a great deal of refining. Sometimes only the fires of affliction will detect the impurities in our hearts so that they may be drawn off by the divine Refiner."[1]

---

[1] Sinclair B. Ferguson, *Maturity: Growing Up and Going On in the Christian Life*, p. 157

Section Three

When in Fear – Look to Jesus

"Therefore lift your drooping hands and strengthen your weak knees, and make straight paths for your feet, so that what is lame may not be put out of joint but rather be healed."

Hebrews 12:12, 13

Chapter Nine

Recognition and admission

*"Let us test and examine our ways, and return to the
LORD."*

Lamentations 3:40

My eyes well up today as I see all the wickedness around me and I begin to think upon Your saving and sanctifying grace. Oh that I would look to You ever so increasingly, for when I think to draw near, I cannot help but eagerly await for the *"blessed hope, the appearing of the glory of our great God and Savior Jesus Christ"*[1] - *"Come, Lord Jesus!"*[2]

When I think of Your truth given to me, I cannot help but wonder why I allow fear to creep in and arise in my heart.

---

[1] Titus 2:13

[2] Revelation 22:20

> *"…for God gave us a spirit not of fear but of power and love and self-control."*[1]

When I really start to investigate my situation, the answer seems always to come back the same – my vision is gazing somewhere else. And how often I find that the majority of the time the fear is not due to some close line of death nor due to severe persecution chasing me down, but rather it is my eyes have wandered onto secondary things.

Lord, it is here that I must *"test and examine"* my ways before You; it is here where I must come to some realization and admission that I have allowed fear to creep in and my sight to veer. For if I am not alert and discerning to recognize my condition, fear would be more than willing to steer me down paths of its repercussions and enslavement, the very vices of Satan. And if I allow fear to take its ugly root, will I not then become like the drowning man who is panicking and flailing and incapable of sound reason? – this of course is to Satan's liking. For he would have me to be in such a state so that I would begin to think wrongly of You and Your character and not turn back to You; or maybe I would act in unrighteous anger and with harsh words; or maybe yet I would act to find answers in mankind hoping for some temporal relief; or maybe I would act out in a shear running headlong into the enjoyments of the flesh and sin, alcohol and drugs, sexual pleasures and instant gratifications. The list goes on to what a man will do to flee from his dark fear. Oh Lord, help me to

---

[1] 2 Timothy 1:7; sometimes translated *'sound mind'* where it says *'self-control'*.

always cut off the '*dragon's head*' of fear by keeping me alert and in Your word, in prayer and in locking my sights on You.

Not only should I examine my way, but shall I not also do serious business regarding examining my true position with You,[1] and then I should *return* to You? Oh, by grace, yes! Forgive me, oh Lord, if I have sought to serve two masters, for I cannot live in such a way.[2]

I cannot enter the narrow gate and then seek to walk the easy way.[3] Nor can I expect to be victorious, if like Peter,[4] I take my eyes off of You and become overwhelmed by fear as I stare towards the storms and trials of this life. For what am I gazing upon[5] and what treasures am I storing up and holding dear?[6] Do you not take care of the birds? Am I not of greater value? Can I add a single hour to my life? Do you not clothe the fields with beauty? Is it not You who upholds and takes care of such things? Oh Yes! So why then shall I let anxiousness and worry and doubt and fear take root? Could it be that I have at times, over these last twenty years, taken Your sovereignty lightly and become prey to faulty thinking? Praise You mighty God that You will never leave me nor forsake me![7] I agree with what John Newton said long ago,

---

[1] 2 Corinthians 13:5

[2] Matthew 6:24

[3] Matthew 7:12, 14

[4] Matthew 14:30

[5] Matthew 6:22

[6] Matthew 6:19-21

[7] Hebrews 13:5, 6; Deuteronomy 31:6-8

"I am not what I ought to be, I am not what I want to be, I am not what I hope to be in another world; but still I am not what I once used to be, and by the grace of God I am what I am."[1]

What then shall I say to these things? Praise You God that You are faithful and powerful to redirect my paths, grant me repentance[2] yet again, and daily give me new mercies; You get sweeter and sweeter as You rekindle my desires to walk earnestly, humbly, and powerfully with a contrite heart, oh how wonderful Your salvation and how amazing Your grace!

Yet, Lord, if I say that I love Your grace and long for Jesus, then shall I not also be changed in my thinking, in my response, in my private life and my inner and outer strivings? – Oh, my yes! Your *word is active and sharp*[3] so let me here heed, let me here see and hear, let me here understand and apply Your true grace and emphasize such working realities:

"For the grace of God has appeared bringing salvation for all people, <u>training us</u> to <u>renounce ungodliness</u> and <u>worldly passions</u>, and to <u>live self-controlled, upright and godly lives</u> in the present age, <u>waiting for our blessed hope</u>, the appearing of the glory of our great God and Savior Jesus Christ, who gave Himself for us <u>to redeem us from all lawlessness</u> and to purify for Himself a people for His own possession who are <u>zealous for good works</u>."[4]

---

[1] also see, 1 Corinthians 15:10
[2] not unto salvation over again, rather walking rightly and truly
[3] Hebrews 4:12
[4] Titus 2:11-14

In the light of Your truths, I must ask myself, are these the marks that I bear in my heart, in my mind and on my actions behind closed doors? For I must examine myself here; I must come to admit and submit here; for it is here where fear builds off of my disobedience and unwillingness to stay the course. For if I run headlong towards ungodliness and worldly passions, then it should be to me no wonder that I stumble and fall when I should be running and winning. Oh Lord, may the words of David, be my prayer:

"Who can discern his errors? Declare me innocent from hidden faults. Keep back your servant also from presumptuous sins; let them not have dominion over me! Then I shall be blameless, and innocent of great transgression. Let the words of my mouth and the meditation of my heart be acceptable in Your sight, O LORD, my rock and my redeemer."[1]

Have I, because of fear, sought to be a *"cursed fool"* or a *"blessed man"*?[2] Am I true in my walk with You or am I laying claim to You by fruitless works?[3] Search my heart, make it known to me, let me know before I am utterly broken and then lift me up again. I know, oh Lord how I know, that my fear has more to do with my faulty vision and wrong hopes that I care to admit.

"We are inclined to a sinful trust and dependence upon each other, and to an inordinate fear and dread of each other. We act as if the creature were a god rather than a man, a spirit

---

[1] Psalm 19:12-14
[2] Jeremiah 17:5-9
[3] Matthew 7:21-23

rather than flesh. Thus, our fear magnifies and exalts the creature, putting it (as it were) in God's room and place. God rebukes this sin in His own people: 'I, even I, am he that comforteth you: Who art thou, that thou shouldest be afraid of a man that shall die, and of the son of man which shall be made as grass; and forgettest the LORD thy maker?' (Isa. 51:12–13a). It is evident that fear exalts people and belittles God. It thinks upon a person's harmful power so much that it forgets God's saving power. In this way, a mortal worm, which perishes as the grass, eclipses the glory of the great God, who stretched forth the heavens and laid the foundations of the earth."[1]

Lord, it all must start, that is the killing of my fears and yes salvation itself, with You awakening me to the reality that I have let such take deep root. However, You are the good and faithful vine dresser, so I ask You Lord, may I abide in You.[2] May I always be alert, prepared and washed by Your word, that I might be quick to recognize and admit worldly fear; may I examine my condition, my eyes and my path, and then return speedily to You alone.

"If we were to understand how dear we are to God, our relation to Him, our value in His eyes, and how He protects us by His faithful promises and gracious presence, we would not tremble at every appearance of danger."[3]

---

[1] John Flavel, *Triumphing Over Sinful Fear*
[2] John 15:1-11
[3] John Flavel, *Triumphing Over Sinful Fear*

Lord, You are love;[1] You are perfect;[2] and Your *perfect love casts out all fears*.[3] *"This God – His way is perfect; the word of the LORD proves true; He is a shield for all those who take refuge in Him."*[4] Lord my God, could it very well be, not only because of my wayward vision, but more deeply, that I really do not believe? Could it be that I do not really believe that You can be trusted in and with all things, all matters? Could it be that I have not been trusting and resting in You? – Oh, how You know, You know oh Lord! Help my unbelief.[5]

And Lord, please never let me to forget, nor take lightly, that *the mind set on the flesh is death, but to set the mind on Your Spirit is life and peace. For the mind that is set on the flesh is hostile towards You.*[6] For if I am then in the flesh, that is looking and steering my gaze and desires towards such, I *cannot please You.*[7] Oh Lord, never, please never, let this be my position. Oh how true it is of You and Your word, for if I should desire You to draw near to me, I must draw near to You,[8] putting away a mind that is constantly searching out the flesh. However, being reminded again, it is impossible to draw near to You, pleasing You, should I act faithlessly and unbelieving that You really do not reward me[9] Oh Lord, You know how in my early days, and sometimes even now, to

---

[1] 1 John 4:8

[2] Matthew 5:48

[3] 1 John 4:18

[4] Psalm 18:30

[5] Mark 9:20-25

[6] Romans 8:6, 7

[7] Romans 8:8

[8] James 4:8

[9] Hebrews 11:6

believe You would reward me, a sinner saved only because of Your wonderful working grace, is just too much and too high of a thing for this poor man's mind. But oh, how I do praise You, for You treat me so kindly, show me my error, empower me to return onto the straight and narrow path, and You reward me by drawing near. Halleluiah! And let me not stop here, for let me not forget to daily pick up my cross and chase after You with a humble and contrite heart, for without humility[1] I shall not see Your grace. Your grace is what saves me and trains me the way I should go – what a beautiful dichotomy.

---

[1] James 4:6; 1 Peter 5:5; Proverbs 3:34

"The men of olden times who wrought well in prayer, who brought the largest things to pass, who moved God to do great things, were those who were entirely given over to God in their praying. God wants, and must have, all that there is in man, in answering his prayers. He must have whole-hearted men through whom to work out his purposes and plans concerning men. God must have men in their entirety. No double-minded man need apply. NO vacillating man can be used. No man with a divided allegiance to God, and the world and self, can do the praying that is needed."[1]

---

[1] E.M. Bounds, *E.M. Bounds on Prayer*

Chapter Ten

Satan's cunning – my deception

"But I am afraid that as the serpent deceived Eve by his cunning, your thoughts will be led astray from a sincere and pure devotion to Christ."

2 Corinthians 11:3

As I come to You in these early morning hours today, I cannot but help to praise You, Oh for You are the King of kings, the Lord of lords and the Great I AM! You are so very worthy to be worshipped in all hours, at all times and during all seasons, regardless of plenty or drought, or in peace or turmoil, or when I have the good sense to do so or if I feel nothing. I would not know good, love, grace nor mercy would it not be for You. I also this morning am waiting with eagerness for the hastening of the day when there shall be no more tears, nor sin, nor failures, nor pain, nor wicked governments, nor the despising of Your word. The distractions of this world are so many, to the right and the left, there are just so many paths leading to my destruction.

I am so often reminded of my utter frailties and weaknesses, and just how fallible I am; and here too shall I praise You this day, for in all of this You cause me all the more to look and run to You – so how shall I boast in anything of myself?

Yet, in knowing this, shall I not take heed and caution? Shall I not be alert and prepared? Shall I give too much room for simple knowledge just to be deceived by the deceiver? Even here, if only left to a mental ascent with no applicable understanding, and no wisdom to respond authentically, am I not being deceived by Satan's cunning? A cunning to make things difficult, believe twisted truths, be lost in lies, and in reality be wayward thinking I am walking in truth?

Oh, here I must be watchful and careful not to do two very dangerous things: First, I must be careful, even as I sit here before You, not to give too much of any kind of credit to Satan beyond that of which You have already declared in Your word. Second, I must be careful not to think of myself too highly in any good respects. For Satan cannot be blamed for my disobedience and sin, however, he does stand as my accuser and does too often use the *old man*, that being my past sin nature, to deceive my thoughts. Having said this plainly, I believe it is good for me to be reminded of some simple ways that I can easily fall should I not remain at the ready. And should it be a good and gracious thing in Your site that someone may read this, would it also not be good for them as well to be reminded and understand such deceptions? Maybe this will spare some, including me, much failure, much waisted time and much regret over not walking much more closely with You? Oh Lord, may it be! "*…and lead us not into temptation, but deliver us from the evil.*"[1]

Lord, here let me dwell for some time, for I must guard against my own pride, a lifting up and exalting myself in fashions aimed towards selfish, and most devilish, gains, regardless if they be in the spirited-pride of life or personal strengths; either way I must not have even the ounce of credit in my salvation. The evil one is all too ready to encourage me and lift me up in such sinful ways of thinking about myself; even the smallest of things, to behold some power and/or superiority over another is terribly evil. In this way, I am robbed of spiritual power (if such can be said or done), this being the power to overcome the sins and evils that must be fought every day and at any given time. I cannot but help to think of Sceva's seven sons and how they were absolutely humiliated when they could only pretend to have the same authority and power as You gave the Apostle Paul.[2] Lord, does not the prideful arrogance of boasting in myself lead down roads of believing the lies of trusting in works, especially religious works and duties, as being somehow right with You? Does this not lead to eventually making the work the boast and even the trust? Does this not then twist even further into becoming the self-justification and ultimate destruction of the soul?

"*…he* [Satan] *deceives great multitudes about the state of their souls, making them think they are something when they are nothing; and so eternally undoes them; and not only so,*

---

[1] Matthew 6:13
[2] Acts 19:11-20

but establishes many in a strong confidence of their eminent holiness, who are in God's sight some of the vilest of hypocrites."[1]

Who will stand before the Lord and Savior, Christ Jesus Your dear Son, on judgment day and say,

"Lord, Lord, did we not prophesy in Your name, and cast out demons in Your name, and do many mighty works in Your name?"[2]

Will such a man or woman live if their hope and trust and faith rest here? NO. Oh, that cunning evil one! Help me, oh Lord, to never forget such deception that I may not fall.

"…he [Satan] brings it to pass, that men work wickedness under a notion of doing God service, and so sin without restraint, yea with earnest forwardness and zeal, and with all their might. By this means he brings in even the friends of religion, insensibly to themselves, to do the work of enemies, by destroying religion in a far more effectual manner than open enemies can do, under a notion of advancing it. By this means the devil scatters the flock of Christ, and sets them one against another, and that with great heat of spirit, under a notion of zeal for God; and religion, by degrees, degenerates into vain jangling; and during the strife, Satan leads both parties far out of the right way, driving each to great extremes, one on the right hand and the other on the left, according as he finds they are most inclined, or most

---

[1] Jonathan Edwards, *The Religious Affections*, p.19
[2] Matthew 7:22

easily moved and swayed, till the right path in the middle is almost wholly neglected."[1]

Lord, I shall also be reminded that the real battle does not consist in the wrestling *"against flesh and blood, but against the rulers, against the authorities, against the cosmic powers over this present darkness, against the spiritual forces of evil in the heavenly places."*[2] With this being Your word, and I know Your word to be the truth, then I have to ask myself how I could ever think to win such a battle if I am so mesmerized and enthused with the things, the ways and the men of this world? For it truly is the strategy of the evil one to distract me, lie to me, persuade me and to guide me straight away from You, the One True God.[3]

The evil one loves to belittle the good works that You have called me to do while casting doubt into my mind; thus he tries to instill guilt for not doing work that other people are doing. Is he not busy doing such manipulation through media and technology? Oh Lord, how many today are being deceived under a false guilt and heavy hand of Satan in believing such a lie? For I must be wise and admit how easy it is to fall prey to Satan's cunning. I must be aware that he can so easily deceive me to wrongly compare myself to everyone else. Indeed, this is a most heinous and chaining error!

"Away then with all perplexing fears and desponding thoughts: to undertake vigorously, and rely confidently on

---

[1] Ibid. p. 19, 20
[2] Ephesians 6:12
[3] 1 Corinthians 8:6; also see Matthew 28:19

the divine assistance, is more than half the conquest, 'Let us arise and be doing, and the LORD will be with us' (1 Chron. 22:16)."[1]

So then, shall I not follow Your orders to prepare, suit up, stand and wield the battle attire?[2] Oh by *Your armor* that I *"may be able to stand against the schemes of the devil."*[3] And it is to this end that I must *"keep alert with all perseverance, making supplication for all the saints."*[4] Oh, that cunning evil one! Help me, oh Lord, to never forget such deception that I may not fall.

Lord, I shall also be reminded of how the devil tempted Your Son so that I myself would not think that somehow I am all alone when the devil tempts me.[5] Let me not think that such deserts could not be in my future, for if my Lord was so treated by the devil, will I not also be tempted and treated in such ways? Most assuredly! However, I must remember that You will never tempt me;[6] I will so often be tempted by my own selfish desires.[7] You may test me, especially in sanctification and the breaking down of my roots of pride, through a great many means, even means that were meant for evil by the devil. And yet,

---

[1] Henry Scougal, *The Life of God in the Soul of Man*, p. 78
[2] Ephesians 6:10-20
[3] Ephesians 6:11
[4] Ephesians 6:18
[5] Matthew 4:1-11
[6] James 1:13
[7] James 1:14, 15

"Blessed is the man who remains steadfast under trial, for when he has stood the test he will receive the crown of life, which God has promised to those who love Him."[1]

Jesus was tempted in every way like me[2] and yet without sin. What a faithful high priest He is,

"For our sake he made Him to be sin who knew no sin, so that in Him we might become the righteousness of God."[3]

"Consider, that all of your trials and troubles, the calamities and miseries, the crosses and losses that you meet with in this world, is all the hell that ever you shall have : here you have your hell, hereafter you shall have your heaven; this is the worst of your condition, the best is to come."[4]

For because of Your dear Son, the thief who comes to steal, kill and destroy[5] is unable to do so to me,

"The LORD is my light and my salvation; whom shall I fear? The LORD is the stronghold of my life; of whom shall I be afraid?"[6]

And although the devil prowls around like a roaring lion seeking to devour me,[7]

---

[1] James 1:12
[2] Hebrews 4:15
[3] 2 Corinthians 5:21
[4] Thomas Brooks, *The Mute Christian under the smarting Rod*, p. 233
[5] John 10:10
[6] Psalm 27:1
[7] 1 Peter 5:8

"…do not fear those who kill the body but cannot kill the soul. Rather fear Him who can destroy both soul and body in hell. Are not two sparrows sold for a penny? And not one of them will fall to the ground apart from Your Father. But even the hairs on your head are all numbered. Fear not, therefore; you are of more value than many sparrows."[1]

Oh, that cunning evil one! Help me, oh Lord, to never forget such deception that I may not fall.

Lord, shall I not also be reminded of what a burdensome, heavy, hard and destructive load it is to be under the hand of Satan? And yet Satan would say to me that his are but easy, entertaining, fun and popular with others, but herein is the deception. For like Leonard Ravenhill used to so often say, *"Entertainment is the devil's substitute for joy."* So true. I know the burdens of Satan are heavy and full of toil, for as he deceived in the garden, so resulted toil, pain, hardships and many worries over the immediate world.[2] But I want to remind that ancient serpent, it is Your word, oh Lord, where it is said,

"Cast your burden on the LORD and He will sustain you."[3],

and,

"Come to me, all who labor and are heavy laden, and I will give you rest. Take my yoke upon you, and learn from me,

---

[1] Matthew 10:28-31
[2] Genesis 3:17
[3] Psalm 55:22

for I am gentle and lowly in heart, and you will find rest for your souls. For my yoke is easy, and my burden is light."[1]

Satan knows he cannot touch Your child beyond that line he is given,[2] however he most certainly makes it his business to destroy the works of my maturity and witness as a Christian. I am so very thankful for how Jesus intercedes on my behalf[3] and how He prayed for me that past precious time.[4] You have reminded me again of Molly McPherson's prayer at the prayer meeting long ago,

"Lord, I don't want to carry burdens others make for me, nor burdens the devil makes for me, nor burdens the church wants to put on me, nor burdens from myself. But I do want to carry the burdens You make for me."[5]

Oh, that cunning evil one! Help me, oh Lord, to never forget such deception that I may not fall.

Lord, I am sure I could go on and on with all of how Satan's cunning could lead me into being deceived, however, I would find it best to stop with some last general thoughts and spend much more time praising You – even more so privately than in these printed words. Let me be reminded in a general summary of Satan's strategy in his cunning ways.

- He constantly distracts

---

[1] Matthew 11:28-30

[2] Consider Job 1:6-22

[3] Romans 8:34

[4] John 17

[5] Molly McPherson, as told by Leonard Ravenhill in his book, *Revival Praying*, p. 79

- He tries to cause me to not be content in and with Jesus
- He is the author of confusion[1]
- He tries to cause me to forget the truths and faithfulness of You God
- He seeks to destroy all truth
- He causes fear to rise from anyone or anything apart from You
- He does not want me to fear You – that is to truly fear and tremble before grace (not yet saved) and have a deep reverence (fear), respect and awe of You after receiving grace (salvation)
- He desires to cause me doubt and question You
- He gives temporal things, even enjoyments, so that I would ignore eternal realities
- He would love for me to embrace sin and die
- He really hates prayer and my communication, seeking and longing for You
- …and a million more ways he is cunning

But You oh God, You… You are my strength, my portion, my shield.[2]

You have reminded me here, that I am not to pray for being noticed and receiving praise.[3] Oh dear Lord, my God and my good Shepherd, please make these things contained, things said before and things yet to be said, to be true realities that mark my soul; and let these things be edifying to someone; let

---

[1] Consider 1 Corinthians 14:33
[2] Psalm 18:2
[3] Matthew 6:5, 6

not my heart become conceited and puffed up. Oh, please never Lord! You know, Lord, You know; and not only do You know this, You know me and the very intention of my thoughts.

"Satan, the great enemy of God and man, has been too long in quiet and undisturbed possession of the soul to resign his dominion without a strong and a fearful struggle to maintain it. When the Spirit of God knocks at the door of the heart, every ally is summoned by the 'strong man armed' to 'resist' the Spirit, and bar and bolt each avenue to his entrance. All is alarm, agitation and commotion within. There is a danger of being dispossessed, and every argument and persuasion and contrivance must be resorted to, in order to retain the long undisputed throne. The world is summoned to throw out its most enticing bait – ambition, wealth, literary and political distinction, pleasure in her thousand forms of fascination and power – all are made to pass, as in review, before the mind. The flesh exerts its power – the love of sin is appealed to, affection for some long-cherished lust, some long-indulged habit, some 'fond amusement,' some darling taste – these, inspired with new vigour, are summoned to the rescue. Thus Satan, the world, and the flesh, are opposed to the Father, the Son, and the Spirit, in the great work of spiritual regeneration."[1]

---

[1] Octavius Winslow, *The Work of the Holy Spirit*, p. 60, 61

Chapter Eleven

When in darkness – my hope is in You

"Who among you fears the LORD and obeys the voice of his servant? Let him who walks in darkness and has no light trust in the name of the LORD and rely on his God."

Isaiah 50:10

Father, You have been so very good and patient towards me, so much more than anyone could ever know or imagine. You know my struggles, my battles, and my weaknesses, and yet You have such patience and such tender care. Oh, how great is Your love and faithfulness! You hear me Lord, for truly You are *a friend who sticks closer than a brother.*[1]

Lord, You know what darkness has taken captive my mind in the days prior to Your grace, prior to me becoming altogether new in heart, and although the days ahead of me are all numbered,[2] days in this body that walks the earth and still

---

[1] Proverbs 18:24
[2] Psalm 39:4, 139:16

dark days yet to witness, I praise You that You have being continually teaching me that I must look to You above all else. For I must seek You and know You more so that I would always, especially in times of trials and fears, make You my sure trust. My lack, oh Lord, is always and only because of me and not You; for *You do not change[1]* but I am the one *prone to wander, prone to leave the God I love.[2]* And when I feel a lack of sorts, a coldness or dryness of heart, or even a sort of deadness in my desires and emotions to set my face towards You – but You oh God! You again revive me demonstrating Your perfect love, divine grace and unfailing mercies.[3] You answer my cry when I pray: "*Help me and give me a desire, a clean desire, a desire to know You, to read Your word, to be godly and sanctified, to continue and to stand with You.*" You are so very wonderful!

Lord, I have often been reminded of Lot and where it says in Your word:

"*...and if He rescued righteous Lot, greatly distressed by the sensual conduct of the wicked (for as that righteous man lived among them day after day, he was tormenting his righteous soul over their lawless deeds that he saw and heard); then the Lord knows how to rescue the godly from trials...*"[4]

I have often felt something like Lot, my soul ripped up over seeing the rampant wickedness in our land and over my own

---

[1] Malachi 3:6
[2] Hymn, *Come Thou Fount of Every Blessing*
[3] Lamentations 3:22, 23
[4] 2 Peter 2:7-9a

carelessness and lack of true desire for You. Although I find it hard to think of myself as being righteous, I know that through the Lord Jesus Christ alone, by His grace, sacrificial love and atoning propitiation, I too am right with You.[1] And though I can rejoice in this and be ever so thankful, however, I know I cannot be thankful for my right standing alone, for You are the hero in this story above and You are the singular One to whom all thanksgiving is due; it's You who knows how to rescue the godly from temptations, therefore it's You where I must keep my gaze directed.

Lord, I am so thankful for Your word, Your truth and Your witness to the Truth. I am thankful that You reveal Your character, Your great love and focus on Your dear Son Jesus, and that in and by Your Spirit, You teach me to understand and convict me to apply Your inspired truths. I know that darkness lurks all around, and I know there are seasons and reasons to walk through the trials and great difficulties of this *present darkness*,[2] and I praise You how You are teaching me to *trust in Your name and rely upon You*.

"But the LORD GOD helps me; therefore I have not been disgraced; therefore I have set my face like a flint, and I know that I shall not be put to shame.

"He who vindicates me is near. Who will contend with me? Let us stand up together. Who is my adversary? Let him come near to me.

---

[1] 2 Corinthians 5:21; also consider (for starters): Romans 3:21-26, 5:11, 12, 6:17, 18; 1 Corinthians 1:30, 31
[2] Ephesians 6:12

"Behold, the LORD GOD helps me; who will declare me guilty? Behold, all of them will wear out like a garment; the moth will eat them up.

"Who among you fears the LORD and obeys the voice of his servant? Let him who walks in darkness and has no light trust in the name of the LORD and rely on his God.

"Behold, all you who kindle a fire, who equip yourselves with burning torches! Walk by the light of your fire, and by the torches that you have kindled! This you have from My hand: you shall lie down in torment."[1]

Oh Lord, may I never try to *light my own way and with my own source*. Oh, my Lord, may I only look to You alone and increase my reverence and my desire to walk with You amid the darkness of the present day. It is in the darkness of my trials and fears, my difficulties and sufferings, in my desert valleys and dark caves, that I must remember those who walked before me and respond:

"Therefore, since we are surrounded by so great a cloud of witnesses, let us also lay aside every weight, and sin which clings so closely, and let us run with endurance the race that is set before us, looking to Jesus, the founder and perfecter of our faith, who for the joy that was set before Him endured the cross, despising the shame, and is seated at the right hand of the throne of God. Consider Him who suffered from sinners such hostility against Himself, so that you may not grow weary or fainthearted. In your struggles against sin,

---

[1] Isaiah 50:7-11

you have not yet resisted to the point of shedding you blood."[1]

Lord, I never want to be tired of Your word; I never want to be too quick to *pass by* and *move on*; let me dwell here forever and ever as You know and see fit for me. There are just so many truths, so much help, so much victory and so much depth in Your word above.

So when all '*hell*' seems to be breaking out around me, help me Lord to remember, this is not the final hell that awaits the wicked, those who refuse to bow the knee, refuse to acknowledge You now and turn to You. Oh Lord, oh Lord please, save their souls, please Lord, continue and extend Your redemption for those wayward of You. For Lord, You *do not desire any should perish.*[2] Break my heart for what breaks Yours.[3] Help me to remember Your words of hope as well, for even when *my own heart seeks to condemn me, You are greater!*[4] Remind me to ask and be reminded:

"Why are you cast down, O my soul, and why are you in turmoil within me? Hope in God; for I shall again praise Him, my salvation and my God."[5]

And…

---

[1] Hebrews 12:1 4

[2] 2 Peter 3:9

[3] Where I first heard this I cannot remember, however I have heard this quoted by several men.

[4] 1 John 3:20

[5] Psalm 42:5

"The LORD is my light and my salvation; whom shall I fear? The LORD is the stronghold of my life; of whom shall I be afraid?"[1]

Lord, for You are the God of my salvation, my true rock, my refuge, my stronghold, and if indeed this is my reality and my position, then how can I not trust You?

And Lord, let me not be deceived as to the times and season whereby in Your providence I find myself living. Let me be alert, prepared and armed for the true spiritual battle, for then I will not fall prey to Satan's cunning nor his heated demands to back down, bow and be devoured. Help me to hear and see clearly Your words of preparation so that fear would not overwhelm my heart and overtake my abilities to see clearly the narrow way. May I never trust in the arm of the flesh and strength of my own hand. How blessed is Your inspired word, through the Apostle's letter addressed *to all those in Rome who are loved by God and called to be saints*, does He here not address my need in this hour?

"Besides this you know the time, that the hour has come for you to wake from sleep. For salvation is nearer to us now than when we first believed. The night is far gone; the day is at hand. So then let us cast off the works of darkness and put on the armor of light. Let us walk properly as in the daytime, not in orgies and drunkenness, not in sexual immorality and sensuality, not in quarreling and jealousy. But put on the

---

[1] Psalm 27:1

Lord Jesus Christ, and make no provisions for the flesh, to gratify its desires."[1]

Lord, what shall I deduce from this? Shall I not heed now, today, this very hour? Oh, help me to see and to realize the significance, oh Lord. So let me never forget:

i. You have made the time known to me throughout Your Scriptures

ii. The hour, the very time I come to awareness of this truth, that I must wake from spiritual sleep – from being lax and lazy, from being ignorant and prayerless, from allowing too much of the world to infiltrate and saturate.

iii. I first truly believed twenty years ago and now I am closer than when I first believed; not only this, but I am among the closest generation of people ever since the church was born.

iv. Time for sleep has left, the time to be alert, diligent and armed is at hand.

v. I must cast off the works of darkness and the sin which so easily entangles (Hebrews 12:1).

vi. I must put on the armor of light, that being the truth and the very person of Christ Jesus Himself.

vii. I must walk as one walking in the daytime, easily seen, realizing You see everything my God and nothing is hidden from Your sight (Hebrews 4:13).

viii. All the sexual sins must be mortified, along with the quarreling (thus even the online arguing and feeling the necessity to have to give an opinion at every turn)

---

[1] Romans 13:11-14

ix.   Again, I must put on the Lord Jesus Christ Himself, the light which came into the world (John 3:19), for the light exposes all.

x.   I must not make provisions for the flesh, so that I would not fulfill such desires and thereby walk contrary to You.

and jealousy and covenanting anything and everything and everyone.

Oh Lord, make these things to be etched into my mind, tattooed on my heart and burned into my daily life, the very moment by moment time, that I might be alert, aware and responding with sound wisdom. Lord, for if I am living in such a way, not in perfection, but with a burning desire to walk uprightly, how then does fear even have a chance to distract me away from You? However, I must ask myself, do I really, deep down, desire such a walk? Oh Lord, You know. Yes Lord, only You really know. Show me, guide me and let me see the truth of myself and the truth of what I say – for I have got to know. You are faithful and thus I know You will do what is for my eternal best.

Father, when fear does creep in, and I have not been alert, at the ready, having been fully armed, please remind me of Your truths that I would be healed and restored once again. For even if Satan should demand to sift me like wheat, I know that the precious Lord Jesus has interceded for me and granted me an unfailing faith.[1]

---

[1] Luke 22:31, 32

"Let us be often lifting up our hearts toward God; and if we do not say that we love him above all things, let us, at least, acknowledge that it is our duty, and would be our happiness, so to do: let us lament the dishonour done unto him by foolish and sinful men, and applaud the praises and adorations that are given him by that blessed and glorious company above: let us resign and yield ourselves up unto him a thousand times, to be governed by his laws, and disposed of at his pleasure: and, though our stubborn hearts should start back and refuse, yet let us tell him, we are convinced that his will is always just and good; and therefore desire him to do with us whatsoever he pleaseth, whether we will or not."[1]

---

[1] Henry Scougal, *The Life of God in the Soul of Man*, p. 93

Chapter Twelve

Will You find faith in me?

"Nevertheless, when the Son of Man comes, will He find faith on earth?"

Luke 18:8

Almighty God, as I ponder and think over Your word above, I must ask, have You not stamped this on my heart since the day I first read such truth? – And yet, how easy it is for me to forget! Oh Lord, do not ever let me forget nor fail to apply this text and respond. I need to ask myself today:

→ Do You find faith in me today?
→ Will You find faith in me on that day?
→ Will I be found walking on the narrow path being led by Your Holy Spirit?
→ Will I be increased with love, compassion and humility?
→ Or will I be found wandering and wayward?

125

→ Or will what has been written here bear witness against me?

Lord please, I ask of You a thousand times over, and thus praise Your holy name, may I be marked by grace, bruised by love and matured in devotion, prayer and obedience. Lord grant this poor man that I might press in and on, and when Jesus comes, He will find in me a resolve in prayer[1] and a faith persevering for Your glory. For I never want it to be said of me, nor of anyone to whom I can think:

"The harvest is past, the summer is ended, and we are not saved."[2]

I am reminded today, and I cannot help but to agree, with what one preacher recently past often used to say:

"The greatest miracle that God can do today is to take an unholy man out of an unholy world and make him holy, then put him back into that unholy world and keep him holy in it."[3]

Oh Lord, what an amazing miracle it is that *Jesus Christ would shed His own blood for me.*[4] Lord, I never want to cease in my awareness of knowing:

→ You are my greatest need

---

[1] Luke 18:1-7

[2] Jeremiah 8:20

[3] Leonard Ravenhill, heard quoted in several messages, recommend the book, *In Light of Eternity: The Life of Leonard Ravenhill*

[4] Hymns: *On Calvary's Brow My Savior Died* and *Chief of Sinners Through I Be*

→ I need always to be about growing in and by Your word.

→ I must be prepared prior to the trials and fears in walking with You.

→ When the trials come, that I would run to Christ and the example set before me.

→ I need to always be dressed in Your armor.

→ That I would lay down my arms that You might empty me of my selfishness and pride.

→ That I would always be trusting and rejoicing in You.

→ When fear lurks its ugly head, I would recognize and admit my need and set my sights rightly on You again.

→ That I would not be ignorant of Satan's cunning as Your word has declared all I need to know for both wisdom's sake and victory against the evil one.

→ When darkness tempts and persuades me that I have no hope, that You will remind and revive me to delight in You, my rock, my fortress and my strong tower.

You have saved me and carried me these last twenty years, I know, that should You grant me twenty more, You shall carry me all the further. Oh Lord God, You are so beautiful and faithful! Oh, that I may trust You all the more!

Lord, like the *"widow woman"*[1] let me too pray with such tenacity and unfailing resolve; even more so, grant me to learn to pray like Your dear Son Jesus. As it says in Your word:

"In the days of His flesh, Jesus offered up prayers and supplications, with loud cries and tears, to Him who was able to save Him from death, and He was heard because of His reverence. Although He was a son, he learned obedience through what He suffered; And being made perfect, He became the source of eternal salvation to all who obey Him…"[2]

And…

"…He lifted up His eyes to heaven, and said, 'Father, the hour has come; glorify Your Son that the Son may glorify You, since You have given Him authority over all flesh, to give eternal life to all whom You have given Him. And this is eternal life, that they may know You the only true God, and Jesus Christ whom You have sent.'"[3]

And again…

"Holy Father, keep them in Your name, which You have given Me, that they may be one, even as we are one."[4]

Continuing…

---

[1] Luke 18:1-8
[2] Hebrews 5:7-9a
[3] John 17:1b-3
[4] John 17:11b

"I do not ask that You take them out of the world, but that You keep them from the evil one. They are not of this world, just as I am not of the world. Sanctify them in the truth; Your word is truth. As You sent me into the world, so I have sent them into the world. And for their sake I consecrate Myself, that they also may be sanctified in truth."[1]

What deep and profound, extremely encouraging and promising, the words that Jesus prayed. Lord, help me to be so minded, remembering that if Jesus prayed such and He consecrated Himself, I know that I too shall be brought to completion.[2]

And yet in Gethsemane, at the darkest of hours, oh how He prayed.[3] However, let me not miss the warning, for during the same dark hour, three times the disciples fell asleep at the watch.[4] *"Watch and pray that you may not enter into temptation. the spirit indeed is willing, but the flesh is weak."*[5] Let me take heed of this command as well, for is not the hour I am living today not growing ever darker? Indeed.

Father, as You know a dear brother recently said,

"If we are passionate worshipers of Jesus, then everything else is secondary. If Jesus is the primary object of our passions, then everything else becomes the by-product. If we ever get that wrong, we cease to be effective. If soul winning

---

[1] John 17:15-19

[2] Philippians 1:6

[3] Matthew 26:36-46

[4] Matthew 26:40, 43, 45

[5] Matthew 26:41

is our primary object, we cease to be effective soul winners. If faith is our primary object, then we cannot be faithful. If holiness is our primary object than we cannot be holy. If revival is our primary object, then we will never see revival. Outside of Jesus being the primary object of our lives, then we immediately begin to lose ground in every aspect of our walk, whether we are pastors or teachers or whatever role we have in the Body."[1]

Oh Lord, how true it is that I need You far above all else. You call me to obedience and to work out my *salvation with fear and trembling,*[2] and although the duty, this being the responsibility to read, heed and obey Your word is mine, I know that all the power to do so is Yours. I know Lord, that should I become boastful in myself and sin, there is absolutely no way I could ever repent and truly obey apart from Jesus. So, I ask that you increase my singleness of eye, my knowledge and my desire to be attentive to my duties, and at the same time, increase Your conviction, Your strength and Your faith in me.

"Do you mortify; do you make it your daily work; be always at it whilst you live; cease not a day from this work; be killing sin or it will be killing you. Your being dead with Christ virtually, your being quickened with him, will not excuse you from this work."[3]

And should not one of the most important duties, at least to the degree You have called of me in Your providence and

---

[1] Frank Mceleny, Christian Author and Blogger

[2] Philippians 2:12

[3] John Owen, *Of the Mortification of Sin in Believers*, p. 9

sovereign will, be that of edifying my brothers and sisters in Christ that they too may be lifted high, walking sure and set towards You? For I never want to be like Cain, when he so carelessly answered you, *"Am I my brother's keeper?"*[1] However to the contrary, shall I not *bear one another's burdens, and so fulfill the law of Christ?*[2] Shall I not *consider others greater than myself?*[3] Shall I not pray like Elisha prayed for his servant's eyes to be opened that he might see Your realities for the facing battle?[4]

"So the LORD opened the eyes of the young man, and he saw, and behold, the mountain was full of horses and chariots of fire all around Elisha."[5]

And should I not intercede for my brothers and sisters like the Apostle Paul did for the Colossians?

"And so, from the day we heard, we have not ceased to pray for you, asking that you may be filled with the knowledge of His will in all spiritual wisdom and understanding, so as to walk in a manner worthy of the Lord, fully pleasing to Him, bearing fruit in every good work and increasing in the knowledge of God. May you be strengthened with all power, according to His glorious might, for all endurance and patience with joy, giving thanks to the Father, who has

---

[1] Genesis 4:9

[2] Galatians 6:2

[3] Philippians 2:3

[4] 2 Kings 6:8-23

[5] 2 Kings 6:17

qualified you to share in the inheritance of the saints in light."[1]

And should I not pray unashamed with tears and loud cries and in much hidden devotion like the Lord Jesus Christ? – Oh, to be with Christ in the school of prayer![2] And shall I not also pray for the lost, for there is *more joy in heaven over one who is lost and turns unto You and is saved than the ninety-nine* who do not need to be rescued.[3]

Shall I not be like Nehemiah?

- What did he hear?
  - "*...the remnant there in the province who had survived the exile is in great trouble and shame. The wall of Jerusalem is broken down, and its gates are destroyed by fire.*"
- What was his response?
  - "*As soon as I heard these words I sat down and wept and mourned for days, and I continued fasting and praying before the God of heaven.*"
- What did he say (part)?
  - "*...confessing the sins of the people of Israel, which we have sinned against You. Even I and my father's house have sinned. We have acted very corruptly against You and have not kept the commandments, the statues, and*

---

[1] Colossians 1:9-12
[2] Consider Andrew Murray's book, *With Christ in the School of Prayer*
[3] Luke 15:7

> *the rules that you commanded your servant Moses."*

Should I not pray with depth and be willing to admit and confess the same?

Does not all of this really come down to love?

> *"So now faith, hope, and love abide, these three; but the greatest of these is love."*[1]

Yet here this may very well be one of the greatest areas I have been disobedient, even downrightly set against in the recesses of my heart, over the last several years of my Christian life. And why? I remember the very year, the place, the time of day where You made it so very plain to me – for You instructed me, with Your gentle conviction and encouragement, that I was to pursue, read, study and search out Your great love and to begin down that path of walking, praying and thinking.

However, I did not do this. Lord, here I must seek Your forgiveness; here in this detail I must turn back to You yet again; here I must make this my precious and joyous labor; for today I am reminded of this and my need to speak it forth here and now.

And yet, what do You give me in return? Such unbelievable forgiveness, lasting hope, deep excite and blessings upon blessings! What? Blessings? Oh yes, You have given me tremendous blessings – chiefly and namely – Yourself, Your precious Son and Your most blessed Holy Spirit. Oh, for unto

---

[1] 1 Corinthians 13:13

me this day, this night, this early morning, this very hour, You have delighted to vindicate me yet again, by Your mercies, and give me *grace upon grace*,[1] of which is far beyond anything I could deserve, comprehend or verbalize. May all who read this overflow with joyous thanksgiving as well!

So Lord, with these tiny, meager, and completely insufficient words, may I praise You and extol Your name; let me be found in such a way when Jesus comes back or at the last of my days in this temporal temple. May anyone and everyone, those who know You and those who don't yet know You, all who read this simple entreaty and walk with You, be ever so encouraged and empowered to lift their heads up and gaze forevermore unto You.

Oh, that the secondaries and insignificant areas of my life would be put in their correct places, with all self-control and wisdom, so that You would be seen correctly as most magnificent above all else. Lord, to You be the glory, the power and the praise. Lord, *when the Son of Man comes, will He find faith on earth?* In me and all who read, may the answer be an astounding – YES!

"'Surely I am coming soon.' Amen. Come, Lord Jesus! The grace of the Lord Jesus be with all. Amen."[2]

---

[1] John 1:16
[2] Revelation 22:20, 21

"The realization of the Divine presence is the inflexible condition of a right engagement of spirit in the exercise of private prayer."[1]

---

[1] David M. M'Intyre, *The Hidden Life of Prayer*, p. 24

Bits of Gold

"But He knows the way that I take; when He has tried me, I shall come out as gold."

Job 23:10

In this chapter I would like to share with my readers some *bits of gold* that others have shared with me over the years. I have read these and mulled them over time and again, so much so I cannot remember the count. Some of these were shown to me through other men's preaching, some through reading and some through brothers whom I have been privileged to know and call dear brothers in the faith. And although there are so many thousands more I could have added here, these stand out in my mind and are often with me during my day. I hope and pray they may take root in your soul and lead you into a closer walk with God, a more devoted life to Christ Jesus and in obedience, and power of the blessed Holy Spirit. Amen.

Only expected person

"In all the history of the world Jesus emerges as the only 'expected' person. No one was looking for such a person as Julius Caesar, or Napoleon, or Washington, or Lincoln to

appear at the time and place that they did appear. No other person has had his course foretold or his work laid out for him centuries before he was born. But the coming of the Messiah had been predicted for centuries. In fact, the first promise of his coming was given to Adam and Eve soon after their fall into sin. As time went on various details concerning his person and work were revealed through the prophets; and at the time Jesus was born there was a general expectation throughout the Jewish world that the Messiah was soon to appear, even the manner of His birth and the town in which it would occur having both clearly indicated."[1]

The Father's bargain with Christ for you

In the later 1600's John Flavel wrote this picture of God the Father talking with His dear Son regarding the hopeless and sinless state.

"Here you may suppose the Father to say, when driving his bargain with Christ for you.

"Father—*'My son, here is a company of poor miserable souls, that have utterly undone themselves, and now lie open to my justice! Justice demands satisfaction for them, or will satisfy itself in the eternal ruin of them: What shall be done for these souls?' And thus Christ returns.*

---

[1] Loraine Boettner, *The Person of Christ*, p. 42, 43

"**Son**—'O my Father, such is my love to, and pity for them, that rather than they shall perish eternally, I will be responsible for them as their Surety; bring in all thy bills, that I may see what they owe thee; Lord, bring them all in, that there may be no after-reckonings with
them; at my hand shalt thou require it. I will rather choose to suffer thy wrath than they should suffer it: upon me, my Father, upon me be all their debt.'

"**Father**—'But, my Son, if thou undertake for them, thou must reckon to pay the last mite, expect no abatements; if I spare them, I will not spare thee.'

"**Son**—'Content, Father, let it be so; charge it all upon me, I am able to discharge it: and though it prove a kind of undoing to me, though it impoverish all my riches, empty all my treasures, (for so indeed it did, 2 Cor. 8: 9. "Though he was rich, yet for our sakes he became poor") yet I am content to undertake it.'

"Blush, ungrateful believers, O let shame cover your faces; judge in yourselves now, has Christ deserved that you should stand with him for trifles, that you should shrink at a few petty difficulties, and complain, this is hard, and that is harsh? O if you knew the grace of our Lord Jesus Christ in this his wonderful condescension for you, you could not do it."[1]

---

[1] John Flavel, *Opens the Covenant of Redemption betwixt the Father and the Redeemer*, Volume 1, Sermon 3

All the keys?

"Sixteen years ago I was a minister in a Midland town in England, not at all happy, doing my work for the pay I got, but holding a good position amongst my fellows. Hudson Taylor (famous missionary to China) and two young students came into my life. I watched them. They had something I had not. Those young men stood there in all their strength and joy.

I said to Charles Studd (another well-known missionary):

"What is the difference between you and me? You seem so happy, and I somehow am in the trough of the wave."

He replied:

"There is nothing that I have got which you may not have, Mr. Meyer."

But I asked:

"How am I to get it?"

"Well," he said,

"Have you given yourself right up to God?"

I winced. I knew that if it came to that, there was a point where I had been fighting my deepest convictions for months. I had lived away from it, but when I came to the Lord's table and handed out the bread and wine, then it met me; or when I came to a convention or meeting of holy people, something stopped me as I remembered this. It was the one point where my will was entrenched. I thought I would do something with Christ that night which would settle it one way or the other, and I met Christ.

I knelt in my room and gave Christ the ring of my will with the keys on it, but kept one little key back, the key of a closet in my heart, in one back story in my heart.

He said to me:

"Are they all here?"

And I said:

"All but one."

"What is that?" said He.

"It is the key of a little cupboard," said I, "in which I have got something which Thou needest not interfere with, but it is mine."

Then, as He put the keys back into my hand, and seemed to be gliding away to the door, He said:

"My child, if you cannot trust Me with all, you do not trust Me at all."

I cried:

"Stop!"

...and He seemed to come back; and holding the little key in my hand, in thought I said:

"I cannot give it, but if Thou wilt take it Thou shalt have it."

He took it, and within a month from that time He had cleared out that little cupboard of things which had been there for months. I knew He would. May I add one word more? Three years ago I met the thing I gave up that night, and as I met it I could not imagine myself being such a fool as nearly to have sold my birthright for that mess of pottage.

I looked up into the face of Christ and said:

"Now I am thine."

For if we desire to have that which we know we do not have, we can have it, but we must ask and we must surrender all. And if we will surrender all, then we too will have the peace, love, and joy of Christ. Just think how many people could be affected by the outcome."[1]

Velvet mouthed preacher

"I'll tell you a story. The Archbishop of Canterbury in the year 1675 was acquainted with Mr. Butterton the actor. One day the Archbishop . . . said to Butterton . . . 'pray inform me Mr. Butterton, what is the reason you actors on stage can affect your congregations with speaking of things imaginary, as if they were real, while we in church speak of things real, which our congregations only receive as if they were imaginary?' 'Why my Lord,' says Butterton, 'the reason is very plain. We actors on stage speak of things imaginary, as

---

[1] F.B. Meyer, *The Christ-Life for the Self-Life*

if they were real and you in the pulpit speak of things real as if they were imaginary.'"

"Therefore," says Whitefield, "I will bawl, I will not be a velvet-mouthed preacher."[1]

Concerning tears and humility

"My eyes will flow without ceasing, without respite, until the LORD from heaven looks down and sees; my eyes cause me grief at the fate of all the daughters of my city."[2]

Leonard Ravenhill used to often say regarding preaching hard and with strong zeal, *"Weep before You whip."*

Ravi Zacharias used to often tell his young colleagues and preachers, *"Humble in heart; wise in response."*

My dear friend and brother in Christ told me when he was pastoring a small church he had to go and confront a man in the church who was in grievous sin against God and his

---

[1] Harry S. Stout, *The Divine Dramatist: George Whitfield and the Rise of Modern Evangelicalism*, p. 239–240 (*This book I do not recommend, rather consider reading, *George Whitefield's Journals*, The Banner of Truth Trust; *George Whitefield: The Life and Times of the Great Evangelist of the Eighteenth-Century Revival*, by Arnold Dallimore)

[2] Jeremiah, Lamentations 3:49-51

family. He took with him a brother, and long-time missionary to some of the darkest and deadliest places on the earth, to be witness and aid in this man's repentance. My friend told me that he confronted him and talked much with the man, yet the man remained stone cold. It was when the missionary started to weep over the man's condition, praying and pleading with man, that this man broke down, genuinely repented, seeing his great sin and need for God's grace. My friend told me, "*I brought with me the truth of the Scriptures, but Kevin brought with it tears.*" I shall never forget this lesson.[1]

"In my twenties, during a period of pastoring, I loved to go past the Salvation Army building, which was the largest one outside of London. There's a huge block of stone at the front. Chiseled in one stone it says, '*William Booth of the Salvation Army opened this corps*', and then it gives the date of 1910. In a second stone it says, '*Kate and Mary Jackson, officers in this corp.*'

"It was in this poor city, where they spin and weave cotton into cloth and the whole town was on the poverty level, that Kate and Mary Jackson labored for a couple of years and nothing happened. Those girls worked diligently and went to bed exhausted at night.

"So they wrote William Booth: '*Would you kindly move us to another station? We're so tired and disheartened. We've tried everything that we've been taught to do. Please move us to another location.*'

---

[1] Brian Long, Itinerant Preacher. The missionary: Kevin Turner of *Strategic World Impact*.

"Booth sent a telegram back with two words – '***Try tears***.' They did and they saw real revival come. Those girls went to travailing prayer – not just prayer, but travailing prayer, prayer with anguish in it. The road to revival is often paved with tears and brokenness."[1]

---

[1] Leonard Ravenhill, *In Light of Eternity: The Life of Leonard Ravenhill* by Mack Tomlinson, p. 15

Biography

Jeff R. Bys is a Christian, husband, father to many and missionary. Jeff's wife, Stephanie, serves alongside loving, caring for, and serving the children, staff and local peoples of Mercy Home. Including these roles, Jeff is also the Director of Mercy Ministries – AFM Africa, AFM Board Vice Chairman and is the pastor of Mercy Baptist Church. Before going to Africa, Jeff worked in the corporate world in Texas.

Jeff says, "I feel like if the Apostle Paul and John Bunyan were with us today, I would want to debate them over who the chief of sinners really is. I am such a poor servant of Christ that I do not even know the day in which salvation came to me. But I do know that in the mercy of God, it has surely come. God is everything, and I am nothing. It is with a great awareness that I sing of the Rock of Ages along with Toplady, *"Nothing in my hands I bring, simply to Thy cross I cling."* It is with this truth in mind that I live each day. I deserve death and wrath, but God allows me to live in Kaya village and be a father to over 100 children. I deserve hell, but God has given me 17 years and counting with my beautiful bride Stephanie. I deserve condemnation, but God allows me to preach His glorious Gospel to His church, His school, and His children's home in the village of Kaya in western Kenya. *Soli Deo Gloria!"*

Jeremy B. Strang | During May of 2001 Jeremy's life was drastically changed. The many years of darkness and bondage that he experienced was brought headlong into the light of Jesus Christ. Painting a picture of his life before Christ, he says, "*I was living in a hellish deep dark depression, one very hidden, and controlling of my life. As a result, this helped to fuel my pride, empower my anger and enslave me in lust. I was a liar, a thief, an adulterer, a drunk, a malicious gossip and a flat-out God hater. I used profanity as communication, anger as a lifestyle, all while deceitfully justifying myself. I lived with thoughts so dark and so wicked, it was as if hell itself lived inside my mind. Nearly every day suicide swirled about my head. This was my reality.*"[1]

Jeremy is a Christian, a husband, and a father. Recently he started studying Theology and Pastoral Studies through the London Reformed Baptist Seminary (Metropolitan Tabernacle) and continues to work full-time in the Radiology field. He also serves on the board of directors for AFM Ministry and has volunteered with various ministries over the past two decades. Jeremy has several other books which can be downloaded at: http://ASimpleWalk.com

---

[1] *Grace Upon Grace*, Jeremy B. Strang

"Sometimes, when I see some of the worst characters in the street, I feel as if my heart must burst forth in tears of gratitude that God has never let me act as they have done! I have thought, "If God had left me alone, and had not touched me by His grace, what a great sinner I would have been! I would have run to the utmost lengths of sin, dived into the very depths of evil. Nor would I have stopped at any vice or folly, if God had not restrained me!

"I feel that I would have been a very king of sinners, if God had left me alone. I cannot understand the reason why I am saved, except upon the ground that God would have it so. I cannot, if I look ever so earnestly, discover any kind of reason in myself why I should be a partaker of Divine grace."

~ Charles Spurgeon ~